DEVELOPING 007

FROM THE BOOKS OF IAN FLEMING TO THE FILMS OF ALBERT R. BROCCOLI

VOLUME I

BICEP BOOKS
Roswell, New Mexico, U.S.A.

ISBN- 978-1-953221-11-7

DEVELOPING 007

FROM THE BOOKS OF IAN FLEMING TO THE FILMS OF ALBERT R. BROCCOLI

VOLUME I

JOHN LEMAY

Danish first edition of *Casino Royale*.

For Neil Riebe, James Bond fan extraordinaire
and the "M" of my writing world.

BOND
7

CONTENTS

INTRODUCTION

When comparing Albert R. Broccoli to Ian Fleming in terms of 007's longevity, it's a bit like the case of the chicken and the egg. Not, of course, which one came first, but which one was more crucial to James Bond's enduring popularity? Perhaps it's a cheat of an answer, but I would say both are of equal importance. There would be no Bond to begin with without Fleming, but without Broccoli, chances are I and many others would've never even heard of 007. If not for the films, it's possible Bond would have rated only as a literary pulp hero that had his moment in the sun and then faded into the dog-eared pages of obscurity. I say this because even though I've been a Bond fan since I was ten years old—and have seen each of the films many times—I did not until recently read Fleming's novels.

I would guess that if you're reading this book, you already know who Ian Fleming and Albert R. Broccoli are, by the way. But, for a brief refresher for anyone who might need it, Ian Lancaster Fleming was born May 28, 1908, and during WWII worked for Britain's Naval Intelligence Division. As such, Fleming had firsthand experience in the world of spies and espionage, notably planning Operation

Goldeneye, among other operations.[1] Fans of the movies will naturally make the connection to 1995's *Goldeneye* right away, while more knowledgeable fans will already know that Goldeneye was the name of Fleming's home in Jamaica. Fleming lived at Goldeneye three months out of every year and wrote his first Bond novel, *Casino Royale,* there out of boredom and nervousness as he waited to get married to Ann Charteris in the winter of 1952.[2]

Ian Fleming pictured in between Harry Saltzman (left) and Albert R. Broccoli (right).

Casino Royale was successful enough to warrant sequels, each of which was often more profitable than the last. Bond got an added boost in March of 1961 when *Life* listed Fleming's fifth 007 novel, *From Russia, with Love,* among President John F. Kennedy's favorite books. A few months later in June of that same year, film producer Harry Saltzman and his EON Productions bought the film rights to all the existing James Bond novels but *Casino Royale,* which had already been purchased by another producer.

---

[1] Operation Goldeneye was an Allied effort to monitor Spain to keep tabs on a possible alliance between Francisco Franco and the Axis powers of WWII.

[2] It should be noted that Fleming wasn't a novice and wrote regularly for *The Sunday Times*. In many instances, assignments for the *Times* gave him plot ideas for the 007 novels.

Saltzman was planning on adapting *Thunderball*, the most recent Bond novel, but it proved too difficult to get off the ground. Saltzman was soon approached by Albert R. Broccoli, who wanted to purchase the Bond rights from him. Not wanting to part with them, Saltzman instead formed a partnership with Broccoli, and the duo decided to produce *Dr. No* as it was less ambitious.

As we all know, the relatively low-budget film was a success that led to a follow-up, *From Russia with Love,* in 1963, which opened the door for the all-out mania that was 1964's *Goldfinger*. The next year's *Thunderball* was even more epic, and Bond movies have been big events ever since. However, the franchise wasn't without its ups and downs. The first bump in the road was Sean Connery's exit from the role after 1967's *You Only Live Twice*. That same year also saw the disastrous comedy version of *Casino Royale*.

Albert R. Broccoli poses for a publicity photo with Roger Moore and Barbara Bach for *The Spy Who Loved Me* (1977).

Broccoli and Saltzman would eventually find a proper replacement for Connery in the form of Roger Moore upon

1973's *Live and Let Die*. During filming of *The Man with the Golden Gun* in 1974, Broccoli and Saltzman's partnership, which had been tenuous for a while, finally reached its breaking point. It resulted in a three year wait for the next Bond film, produced solely by Broccoli: 1977's *The Spy Who Loved Me*. The production was also notable for having nothing in common with the novel of the same name other than the title itself and a steel-toothed villain. As it turned out, this would become the norm for Broccoli's Bond films from then on, with 1979's *Moonraker* being one of the last ones to stick relatively close to its source material. By the 1980s, and still lacking the rights to *Casino Royale*, Broccoli had to resort to adapting Fleming's short stories into feature films, the first of which was 1981's *For Your Eyes Only*. Actually, the film was based upon two short stories: "For Your Eyes Only"—about a beautiful young woman avenging her dead parents—and "Risico"—where Bond gets tangled up with a couple of smugglers. While *For Your Eyes Only* the film retained a few elements from the short stories, future entries, like 1985's *A View to a Kill*, utilized the title and nothing else.

Also surprising is the order of the movies vs. the books. Case in point, in terms of the novels, *You Only Live Twice* is actually the sequel to *On Her Majesty's Secret Service*. In that book, an amnesia-stricken Bond avenges himself upon Blofeld after the death of his wife, Tracy. Just the opposite, *You Only Live Twice* the film has Bond coming face to face with Blofeld for the first time and is followed by *On Her Majesty's Secret Service*, where Blofeld kills Tracy. Likewise, *Dr. No* is actually the sequel to *From Russia, with Love* in terms of the books as well.

Whereas usually films based on books pale in comparison to their source material in terms of grandeur, when it comes to James Bond, it's the reverse. *Moonraker*, the novel, is set entirely in England and pertains to a mad industrialist planning to destroy London with a mega-rocket code-named Moonraker. The globe-trotting film adaptation, on the other hand, actually shoots for the moon and takes 007 into outer space. The same was true of 1967's *You Only Live Twice*, which added in elements of the space race and had Blofeld launching rockets from a hollowed-out volcano. By contrast, the book has Blofeld holed up in a Japanese castle near a volcano sans any space capsules.

As you can see, Fleming's novels and Broccoli's films are completely different animals in most cases. And so is this book when compared to other non-fiction James Bond tomes, usually devoted to the movies rather than the novels from which they originate. As such, this book is both for Bond fans and also for writers, whether burgeoning or already published. Whichever camp you fall into, looking into the creative process of both Ian Fleming and the screenwriters who later adapted his creations is a fascinating process.

Furthermore, this volume is ordered in the sequence of the books, not the movies, since the books came first. I start each chapter with my own brief takeaways of the book and its big screen counterpart, followed by an overview of Fleming's writing process for that particular novel, then a review of the novel with an emphasis on how it differs from its film adaptation.[3] After that, I delve into the developmental process behind the corresponding film, or films plural in the cases of *Casino Royale* and *Thunderball*, both of which had more than one adaptation. I especially highlight discarded screenplay drafts that differed greatly from the final product, including what could be considered lost productions altogether due to how much they differed.[4]

---

[3] I don't bother to provide synopses for the films because if you bought this book, then you probably have a pretty good handle on the films and a synopsis would simply annoy you. The books, on the other hand, I try to offer at least a partial overview of in my reviews.

[4] Over the years, and thanks to books like *Jaws Unmade: The Lost Sequels, Prequels, Remakes, and Rip-Offs*, I've become known as "the lost films guy" in many circles. Naturally, this did start out for me on some level as my "lost Bond movies" book. However, *The Lost*

From one Bond fan to another, and especially to my fellow writers intrigued by the creative process, I hope you enjoy this look into developing 007.

Adventures of James Bond by Mark Editz and the amazingly comprehensive *Scripting 007: Behind the Writing of the James Bond Movies* by Clement Feutry are both already what I consider definitive works on 007's unmade adventures, and I heartily recommend both.

CASINO ROYALE

PUBLICATION DATE: April 13, 1953
ORIGINAL PAGE LENGTH: 213pp.
PUBLISHER: Jonathan Cape

For many years, *Casino Royale* could have been considered the "lost James Bond" movie in several regards, ironic considering that it reigns uncontested as the Bond property with the most adaptations. *Casino Royale* was a lost film in the sense that its original adaptation, a live 1954 teleplay for *Climax!*, went missing for many years. More pertinently, though, it was the one and only Ian Fleming book not to get the EON treatment until the turn of the Millennium, when the production company finally gained the rights.[5]

Worse yet, before the very well-received 2006 film starring Daniel Craig, *Casino Royale* was infamously, and ill-advisedly, adapted as a spoof in 1967. Though fairly well-educated on Bond and knowing what to expect from the spoof, I was no less confused by it when I first saw it at age thirteen. Naturally, I was by then accustomed to all the Bonds from Connery to Brosnan, and while I fully

[5] This was doubly ironic considering the fact that EON had fleshed out short stories like "From a View to a Kill," nothing more than a motorcycle-assassination caper, into full-blown feature films.

appreciated Peter Sellers' Pink Panther films, I was still woefully unprepared for the disaster that unfolded before my eyes.

Though initially discouraging that the property was never adapted in the heyday and Broccoli and Saltzman, the timing ultimately played in the franchise's favor. As it turned out, the 2006 *Casino Royale* was just what 007 needed in the form of a hard reboot. The film was, in my opinion and many others, the best Bond movie ever made.[6] As the first Bond novel, and with no less than three major adaptations, all quite diverse, not to mention an aborted screenplay eyed for 1960s-era-EON, *Casino Royale* constitutes one of the most fascinating developmental processes for a James Bond property ever.

WRITING *CASINO ROYALE*

As they say, you write what you know, and Ian Fleming knew the spy world. *Casino Royale* seemed to flow right out of him, considering he began his first draft on January 17, 1952, and had it finished by March of that same year. In retrospect four years later, Fleming would say he didn't remember why he started *Casino Royale.*[7] In his own words, his "mental hands were empty" in the winter of 1952, and he had by then tired of his daily routine of spearfishing in the waters of Jamaica. Eventually, Fleming more or less admitted that after having been a bachelor for 44 years, he was naturally nervous at the prospect of his impending marriage and needed a distraction, so James Bond was born.

Fleming put quite a bit of himself into the character in both looks and tastes, while also making him a "a compound of all the secret agents and commando types"

---

[6] As such, *Casino Royale* was also the first of Fleming's novels I ever read out of curiosity, though to do this book, I had to read it a second time to refresh my memory.

[7] Other sources noted that he had been itching to write a spy novel for years.

he met during the war.[8] As for other developmental odds and ends, when it came to naming his spy character, Fleming initially called him James Secretan. However, that name was too interesting for Fleming, who wanted the character to have the most boring name that he could imagine, and so he settled on James Bond, in real life the author of *Birds of the West Indies*. In a 1962 article for *The New Yorker*, Fleming explained that initially he didn't envision James Bond as the premiere agent of British Intelligence, but rather "an extremely dull, uninteresting man to whom things happened... when I was casting around for a name for my protagonist I thought by God, [James Bond] is the dullest name I ever heard."[9]

While in future entries, Fleming would often base and name characters after friends, acquaintances, and occasionally people he disliked, in the case of *Casino Royale*, most think that the villain, Le Chiffre, was based upon the occultist Aleister Crowley. (This was particularly evident in the torture scene with the carpet beater.) As for the supporting cast of characters back at Mi6, many of them, like Miss Moneypenny and M, were based on real people in Fleming's life. M, in particular, was modeled after Fleming's own superior, Admiral John Godfrey, and Miss Moneypenny was based on his secretary, Joan Howe, who would later retype the *Casino Royale* manuscript.[10]

On some level, *Casino Royale* required less research than Fleming would do on his sequels. As stated in the introduction, Fleming had worked in Britain's Naval Intelligence Division. *Casino Royale* was probably the closest to Fleming's own war-time exploits working for the Naval Intelligence Division, which stemmed from

---

[8] Macintyre, *For Your Eyes Only*, p.50.

[9] Hellman, "Bond's Creator," *The New Yorker* (April 2, 1962), p.32. In the same piece, Fleming stated, "I wanted him to be a blunt instrument," which is presumably what inspired M to call him a "blunt instrument" in the 2006 *Casino Royale*.

[10] Notably, Miss Moneypenny does not feature into 007's debut adventure.

gambling at the Estoril Casino in Portugal. Fleming and the NID Director, Admiral Godfrey, were on their way to the United States and were on a layover in neutral Portugal. Estoril was reportedly swarming with spies, and Fleming stated that during a game of *chemin de fer* he was cleaned out by a "chief German agent."[11] Contrary to this, Admiral Godfrey claimed that Fleming had merely played against Portuguese businessmen and only told stories about playing against German spies.[12] The only other real-life incident to inspire a scene from the novel, the one where a bomb goes off, was based on the failed assassination of Franz von Papen, Vice-Chancellor of Germany and an ambassador for Hitler. As with the fictional 007, Papen survived the blast only because a grove of trees protected him from the detonation.

"I write for about three hours in the morning ... and I do another hour's work between six and seven in the evening. I never correct anything and I never go back to see what I have written ... By following my formula, you write 2,000 words a day," Fleming said in an article for *Books and Bookmen* magazine in May 1963. This had especially applied to

[11] Lycett, *Ian Fleming*, p.221.

[12] Whether he did or not, Fleming captured the atmosphere of a casino excellently as exemplified in in his novel's opening pages.

Casino Royale, which he pressed on with every day and never looked back. Or, that is to say, he didn't reread his work until the whole manuscript was finished. His reasoning was that grammatical mistakes and a few bad passages may have made him lose heart and his momentum would have ceased. Fleming remembered that he had "savagely hammered" the manuscript out until the "proud day when the last page was done." Fleming continued, "The last line 'The bitch is dead now' was just what I felt. I had killed the job."[13]

Perhaps not coincidentally, he finished the book just in time to marry Ann Charteris on March 24, 1952. As he settled in to married life, he was also faced with the reality of submitting his manuscript to a publisher. Like many first-time authors, Fleming was naturally nervous about how others would perceive his work, which he jokingly called "adolescent tripe." It didn't help matters when an ex-girlfriend suggested that perhaps he should only publish it under a pen name. Fleming decided to test the waters with his friend, British novelist William Plomer, who he told he was "thoroughly ashamed of [*Casino Royale*]."[14]

---

[13] Fleming, *Man with the Golden Typewriter*, p.10.

[14] Nudd, "Ian Fleming & James Bond," *The Book and Magazine Collector* (October 1989), p.4.

As it had happened, Fleming had simply went to lunch with Plomer one day with no intention of asking him to read the book. Or, perhaps he did and breached the subject in a rather coy manner. Fleming had asked Plomer a very specific question regarding prose, to which Plomer stated, "You've written a book." Plomer then convinced Fleming to let him see his manuscript, and the British novelist thought highly enough of it to send it to the publisher Jonathan Cape, whom Plomer occasionally worked for. Ultimately, it was Plomer who got the book published. Jonathan Cape disliked potboilers and thrillers in general, and one of his editors, Michael Howard, positively detested *Casino Royale*. In his mind, it was brutal, sadistic, and too shocking.[15] Plomer pushed the manuscript unrelentingly, and thankfully, it was published. (And in defense of Howard, he would eventually come around to James Bond as the series progressed, and Fleming valued his input.)

A man after my own heart, Fleming horrified his publishers when he dared to design his own cover, organized his own reviews, and marketing tactics. More terrifying, though, was when Fleming would later cast his eagle eye on the company's finances. But Jonathan Cape had scored a winner in Fleming's Bond books. *Casino*

---

[15] Fleming, *Man with the Golden Typewriter*, p.12.

Royale was released on April 13, 1953, and sold out less than a month later, making it a surprise hit.[16] The critical reception was also overall positive, with Hugh I'Anson Fausset of *The Manchester Guardian* calling it "a first-rate thriller" even if it was "schoolboy stuff." After the novel's success, Jonathan Cape offered Fleming a three-book deal, and it was off to the races from there for James Bond, 007.[17]

READING *CASINO ROYALE*

Fleming's first line of prose describing the atmosphere of a casino is both unique and gripping: "The scent and smoke and sweat of a casino are nauseating at three in the morning." It's a strong start to a book that sticks the landing with a blunt, shocking ending passage to boot.

Fleming's Bond is a bit different from his cinematic counterpart. The literary Bond looks like actor Hoagy Carmichael, a detail vocalized in the book by Vesper Lynd. Fleming's Bond also has a vertical scar running down his right cheek, a strand of black hair typically falls just above his right eyebrow, and he's often described as having cold eyes with a cruel mouth in spite of his good looks. This Bond, in his prime in the early 1950s, cherishes a twenty-year-old 1933 4 1/2 litre Bentley, which might seem a departure from the Bond who drives an Aston Martin. Nor is he the superman of the films. Fleming's Bond, while cold

---

[16] To be more specific, the first run consisted of 4,728 copies and a second print run the same month sold out swiftly as well. In the U.S., sales were slower, and Bond wouldn't become a big deal until years later when JFK read *From Russia, with Love*.

[17] Fleming was pleased with Cape's work on *Casino Royale* calling it a "handsome book" that the publisher marketed "superbly." [Fleming, *Man with the Golden Typewriter*, p.34] However, not long after, Fleming would verbally duel with Cape in their correspondence. Their interactions were not unlike Bond's verbal sparring matches with his megalomaniac villains. Ultimately, Fleming got the best of Cape when it came to wit, if not money.

and calculating, is still quite vulnerable to physical and emotional pain. Otherwise, the traits are still all there, including the constant womanizing, gambling, and drinking.[18]

This paperback reissue of *Casino Royale* was notably retitled *You Asked For It* for the U.S. market as an experiment since initially the novel sold poorly there.

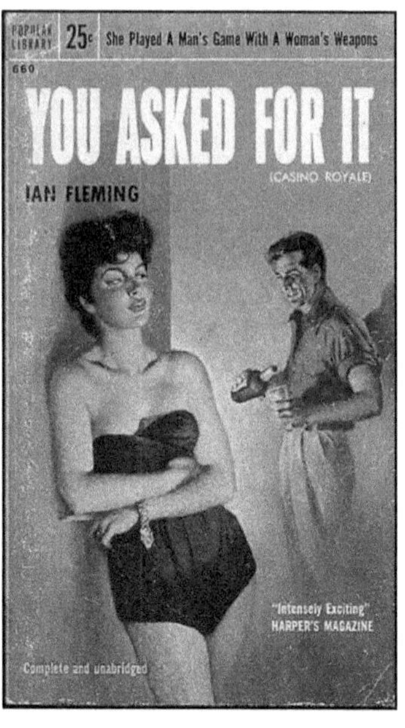

For anyone only familiar with the Daniel Craig film, it should be noted that the novel begins with Bond already in the casino of the title and on his mission. There's not much excitement in terms of action aside from a bomb going off early on, which never made its way into the film. The book has a suspenseful bit the film lacks, though, where one of Le Chiffre's thugs presses a gun concealed in a walking cane against Bond's lower spine under the back of his chair during the game. The thug tells Bond not to bet, and as the dealer preps the game, the tension mounts until Bond gets himself out of the situation by pretending to fall from his chair. The most suspenseful scenes of the 2006 film originate in the book, from Bond's car chase to rescue the kidnapped Vesper to the infamous torture scene with the bottomless chair and the carpet beater.

---

[18] On that note, Bond's famous vodka martini is ordered in the presence of Felix Leiter during their first meeting and the dialogue is somewhat similar to the film. However, in the film, Leiter and Bond meet on the basis of Leiter offering to give him the money to reenter the game. In the book, they've already become fast friends.

Although one may not be able to see the action as in a movie, one thing the books offer that the films can't is Bond's inner monologue and thoughts during such scenes. A good example is Bond's coldness in pursuing Vesper during the car chase and considering not trading her for the money. Then, during the torture scene, Bond reflects on how torture victims sometimes reach a point of sadomasochism, which he hopes he will not succumb to himself out of pride. Reading the scene vs. watching it is just as intense, probably more so. Fleming was famous for his dialogue between Bond and the villain, and since Bond and Le Chiffre never spoke much at the baccarat tables, the infamous chair scene provides their first in-depth conversation. Notably, Le Chiffre chides Bond that this isn't a romantic adventure story where he will be rewarded and get the girl. Perhaps that's why Fleming saw fit to do away with Vesper in the end, so the villain's words would ultimately ring true.

While the carpet beater scene leaves quite an impact, it's still Fleming's splendid description of Bond's gambling habits in the casino that really excels, as does Bond's doomed relationship with Vesper. In a bit of foreshadowing early on, Bond reflects that he has yet to suffer from cards or women, but the day would come. Likewise, Bond is built up as a hard man to work for to Vesper by her boss, who warns her not to fall in love with him—which guarantees that they will. The end section of the novel, where Bond's relationship with Vesper blossoms and spirals out of control, is heart-wrenchingly relatable. While these last few chapters are indeed pulpy, they are no less captivating. Notably, there is no concluding action set piece as in the film, and in the novel Vesper simply takes her own life one night and leaves

Bond a note to explain it all. Though less fantastic than the film version, the novel's ending still packs a punch and sets up future adventures for Bond, with him vowing to tackle SMERSH since they were the ones controlling Vesper. As shocking as it is memorable is Bond's final line, and the last passage of the book, when Bond reports Vesper's death to his superiors: "Yes, dammit, I said 'was'. The bitch is dead now."

AIRDATE: October 21, 1954
RUNTIME: 50 Minutes
DIRECTOR:
William H. Brown Jr.
PRODUCERS: Bretaigne Windust & Elliott Lewis
TELEPLAY: Charles Bennett & Anthony Ellis
MUSIC: Jerry Goldsmith
CAST: Barry Nelson (Jimmy Bond)
Peter Lorre (Le Chiffre)
Linda Christian (Valerie Mathis)
Michael Pate (Clarence Leiter)
William Lundigan (Host)

CLIMAX! CASINO ROYALE ON TV (1954)

In an October 29, 1952 letter to Jonathan Cape, Ian Fleming asked Cape's permission to write to his American agent about *Casino Royale* in hopes that it might become a rip-snorting "marvelous movie." Fleming went on, "No-one has EVER had the bright idea to couple gambling with espionage and economic sabotage and this gimmick ... would film marvelously."[19]

[19] Fleming, *Man with the Golden Typewriter*, p.23.

Still of Barry Nelson as Jimmy Bond and Linda Christian as the composite character of Valerie Mathis.

As the previous passage indicated, Fleming was itching for Bond to become a big screen property before *Casino Royale* had even been published, and to that end, he purchased his own theater agency, Glidrose Productions Limited. In the words of Calvin Dyson on his James Bond YouTube channel, Fleming was "trigger happy" when trying to sell Bond as a film property and I would agree.[20] While Gildrose Productions came to naught, Curtis Brown, Associated British Pictures, and the Music Corporation of America all approached Fleming about a film version. It would be Brown who would eventually bring *Casino Royale* to the small screen as a one-hour, Americanized CBS television adaptation for *Climax!,* an anthology series which ran from 1954 to 1958. Naturally as an anthology, each weekly broadcast presented a different story, adapted from various sources. CBS paid Fleming $1,000 to adapt *Casino Royale*, and the episode, performed live, aired on October 21, 1954.

---

[20] Calvin Dyson, "Casino Royale 1954 Review," YouTube.

All in all, the episode was fairly faithful to the source material. Where it deviated the most was in the characters themselves. Apart from Le Chiffre, all the main players were tweaked in interesting ways. Because it was an American-produced series meant for U.S. audiences, James Bond of Mi6 became Jimmy Bond of the vague "Combined Intelligence" network. (Nor does Nelson's Bond fare well as an American, that's for sure.) Odder yet, it's the Felix Leiter character who is British in this version. (In reality, the roles should have been switched, with Michael Pate playing a British Bond, and Nelson would've been swell as Leiter.) Furthermore, Felix Leiter is essentially combined with René Mathis to become Clarence Leiter, agent for Station S. Mathis is consolidated not only into Leiter but Vesper Lynd as well since her onscreen counterpart, Valerie Mathis, is secretly a French agent posing as one of Le Chiffre's female operatives. For the sake of brevity, she's also retrofitted to become an ex-lover of Bond's, which negated the need for the duo to fall in love in a paltry one-hour time slot already crowded with plot lines.

"Casino Royale" hits the ground running the best that a low-budget TV adaptation can. Replacing the bomb attempt from the book is a shooting as soon as Bond tries to set foot into the casino. (While not at all interesting from a choreography perspective, I suppose it was exciting to see squibs going off during a live performance back in 1954.) Shortly after, Bond meets Leiter for the first time. Actually, the original dialogue isn't that bad, either, with Leiter asking him, "Aren't you the fellow who was shot?" Bond responds, "No, I was the fellow who was missed."

Leiter claims he knows Bond as "Card Sense Jimmy Bond" and asks if he might explain the game of baccarat to him (and thus also the audience). It's actually a rather clever exchange, as Bond more or less pretends to teach Leiter the rules of the game, but when eavesdroppers are out of shot, the real priority takes center stage with Leiter briefing Bond on Le Chiffre.

Barry Nelson at the baccarat table as Bond, far left, and Peter Lorre as Le Chiffre, far right.

Speaking of the big bad, like a primitive precursor of what was to come in the EON films, *Climax!* adds a scene of Valeire introducing Bond to Le Chiffre. Overall, it's similar to future scenes of Bond engaging in pleasant conversation with his enemies in the films. Again, there's no such scene in the book. As for Peter Lorre, though he's certainly villainous, he's not physically intimidating like the literary version of Le Chiffre.

The perennial fly gets stuck in the ointment right before the game, when Bond receives a mysterious phone call warning him that if he wins, Valerie will lose. Bond decides to win anyway, and this leads to another scene from the book where one of Le Chiffre's men points the gun-cane at Bond's spine. The scene was hard to visualize for me in the book, and here it's clumsily acted due to the nature of the live performance. However, live or not, I have a feeling it would have been difficult to stage either way. Bond flips over in his chair to defuse the situation, then shows Leiter the cane like he does Mathis in the book.

Naturally, the producers couldn't go anywhere near the book's infamous torture scene, but they devised a decent compromise. In this scenario, Bond is thrown into a bathtub (fully clothed) to be tortured by way of prying off his toenails. The twist is that Valerie has to watch, and if she loses her nerve and screams, then Bond is to be killed. Actually, this was the only scene where, for me, Nelson actually shined as Bond when he tells Le Chiffre, "You won't get anything out of me. Pain and killing is part of my job." For that matter, it's also Lorre's best scene as Le Chiffre and he does surprisingly well as a Bond villain.

Nor is Bond rescued by SMERSH or Leiter. In this version, Valerie helps him to get free when Le Chiffre and his men have left to go retrieve Bond's winnings. (Valerie caved during the torture scene and told them where Bond hid his money.) When Le Chiffre's men reenter the room, Bond overtakes them, procures one of their guns, and shoots Le Chiffre (offscreen due to TV standards of the day). Le Chiffre doesn't die immediately and manages to grab Valerie, putting a razor blade to her throat. The final moments falter just a bit, as Lorre stumbles over a line along with the choreography when Valerie ducks so Bond can shoot Le Chiffre again. It's just a tad clumsy, but that's live television and it was an admirable effort. Unlike Vesper Lynd, Valerie Mathis falls into Bond's arms in the closing shots, presumably to live happily ever after based on their earlier reconciliation.[21]

For many years, the mini-TV movie that was "Casino Royale" was a lost film. Some sources attest that the original broadcast was in color, though a black and white kinescope of the live broadcast was found by film historian Jim Schoenberger in 1981. According to some, TBS aired it as a curiosity during one of their James Bond movie marathons, making it the first time the *Climax!* version of "Casino Royale" was seen in many years. Notably, it lacked two minutes of content that were still missing, though they

---

[21] An urban legend claimed that Peter Lorre got up before the credits finished rolling creating a blooper, but if one watches the episode this isn't the case.

were thankfully recovered later. The episode was also included on MGM's DVD release of the 1967 *Casino Royale*, and today can be viewed on YouTube.

007'S ABORTED TV SERIES

Interestingly, CBS considered the *Climax!* "Casino Royale" enough of a success that, when combined with 007's rising literary star, in 1958 they approached Fleming about writing a James Bond TV series. Though the series would die before it reached airwaves, it induced Fleming to try his hand at 007 short stories, many of which would form the basis of short story collections and later feature films like 1981's *For Your Eyes Only*. Though CBS desired 32 episodes, it's doubtful that Fleming came up with that many concepts. So far as we know, the aborted episodes resulted in "For Your Eyes Only," "From a View to a Kill," "Quantum of Solace," "Risico," "The Hildenbrand Rarity," "Octopussy," "The Living Daylights," "The Property of Lady," and "007 in New York."

Ben Hecht's *Casino Royale*

The long and meandering road that led to the first big screen adaptation of *Casino Royale* begins with a producer named Gregory Ratoff, who Fleming sold the film rights to in March of 1955 for $6,000.[22] Lorenzo Semple Jr., the future writer of TV's *Batman* and the 1970s spy thriller *Three Days of the Condor,* was commissioned to write a screenplay. Likewise, a January 1956 issue of the *New York Times* reported that Ratoff created a new production company with actor/agent Michael Garrison to produce *Casino Royale*, hopefully to be shot that coming summer.

[22] For those no doubt bemused at modern idea of gender swapping James Bond from man to woman, this idea was contemplated as early as 1956. If some reports are to be believed, Ratoff considered Bond too "stupid" and "unbelievable." For whatever reason in Ratoff's mind, that meant Bond should be gender swapped to become Jane Bond and be played by Susan Hayward! Thankful, this concept never got off the ground. Had the idea gone forth, Bond as we know him may have never made it to the big screen again.

Proposed shooting locations were said to include England, Estoril, and San Remo. Interestingly, the *Times* stated that even though Fleming himself had written a screenplay version, Ratoff wanted a "noted scenarist" to write the script. After Ratoff passed away in December of 1960, the rights to *Casino Royale* were purchased by Ratoff's talent agent, Charles K. Feldman. Before production on *Dr. No*, Albert R. Broccoli tried to purchase the rights from Feldman, who declined. Feldman envisioned adapting the book with his friend, the well-known director Howard Hawks, with Cary Grant to play James Bond. To adapt it into screenplay form, they hoped to get Leigh Brackett. Instead, Feldman ended up hiring the Academy Award-winning screenwriter Ben Hecht, "the Shakespeare of Hollywood," to do *Casino Royale*.

Thankfully, writer Jeremy Duns managed to dredge up the old, neglected screenplay by Hecht, which he found in the Newberry Library in Chicago, where it had been sitting since 1979 accumulating dust. In the folder devoted to *Casino Royale* were found five treatments and screenplays, the first of which was dated 1957 and was not written by Hecht. (It was likely given to him as a starting point for inspiration.) The 1957 treatment would seem to have been inspired by the *Climax!* episode in the sense that James Bond was not only retrofitted to become an American but was replaced entirely by a new American character named Lucky Fortunato. Per Duns, the character wasn't like Bond at all and was a wisecracking card shark gangster. Next came an outline dated December 17, 1963, written after the success of the *Dr. No* movie from EON released that same year. The notes specified that the envisioned scenario would feature sequences taking place in Baghdad, Algiers, and Naples. Like the Bond films from EON, Hecht envisioned a grandiose ending entailing a raid on a German castle.

Not unlike Blofeld's plan to blackmail the world via beautiful women from 1969's *On Her Majesty's Secret Service*, Hecht envisioned Le Chiffre, now a colonel, as running a vast network of brothels. Through beautiful female agents, he obtains delicate information which can be used for blackmail. One of them, in a major new character addition, was to be a former lover of Bond's who also used to be one of Le Chiffre's agents. Other than a few additional scenes, which were needed considering the brevity of the *Casino Royale* novel, Hecht's adaptation was pretty faithful. Notably, one of his endings appeared to be an attempt to dovetail into *Dr. No*. Specifically, according to Duns, after Vesper's suicide, Bond returns to London, where M tells him to take a holiday in Jamaica, though Bond says he'd rather stick to London and wait for another assignment.

After that, Hecht wrote several more screenplays with minor differences, so what follows will be something of a pastiche.[23] For starters, Hecht made a concentrated effort to match the style of the EON films, even going so far as to replace mentions of SMERSH with SPECTRE. Specifically, it was to begin with a pre-credit scene starring Felix Leiter in the process of arresting assorted UN diplomats who fell victim to Le Chiffre's prostitutes. As the story progresses, Bond is teamed with fellow agent Vesper Lynd to take down Le Chiffre, now a SPECTRE operative in charge of the blackmailing operation, instead of SMERSH's banker. Their mission takes them to Hamburg, where Bond runs

[23] One discarded draft will be of particular interest to a subset of 007 fans who like to believe that all of the films are in-continuity with one another. I'm referring to the idea that whenever the old James Bond is killed, he's replaced by a new agent and given the same name and number, thus explaining the switch from Roger Moore to Timothy Dalton, and so on. In this script, perhaps as a way of explaining why Sean Connery might not be playing Bond, Hecht envisioned the movie starting with Bond being dead. M then calls in an American agent to replace Bond and take on his name as a way of confusing the enemy. (Duns noted that this new character was indistinguishable from the old 007 anyways, so why bother?) Hecht went back and forth on the idea, with some drafts containing the real 007 and others the upstart.

afoul of the red light district and reunites with a former lover and current madame, Lili Wing, and her girlfriend, Georgie.[24] (Poor Lili would eventually be fed into a trash compacter by Le Chiffre, while Georgie would pop up again in the last scene.)

One prominent set-piece was to see Bond posing as one of Le Chiffre's eye-patch-wearing henchmen (presumably inspired by the SMERSH operative from the final act of the novel) to steal a van belonging to Le Chiffre. Inside of it are various film reels to be used to blackmail assorted officials. A car chase through the Swiss Alps ensues and concludes with Bond sending the van careening off a cliff. With the film reels destroyed, Le Chiffre's plan is up in smoke. Having lost most of the budget afforded him by SPECTRE, Le Chiffre now needs to recoup his massive losses, which he plans to do at a poker game.

From there the action switches to northern France to the titular Casino Royale. Hecht makes a slight improvement on the book in the sense that by now Bond and Le Chiffre know one another and are arch-enemies. That's because before he destroyed the precious film reels, Bond also led to the disfigurement of Le Chiffre's wife, who Bond used as a human shield during a gunfight. Now Madame Le Chiffre exists as a shell of her former self, with half her face scarred by bullet wounds and a metallic voice due to a damaged larynx and a tube in her throat. Interestingly, Hecht thought he could get away with the infamous ball-busting torture scene from the book. However, he decided that Madame Le Chiffre should be the one to wield the deadly carpet beater to torture Bond while Le Chiffre does the interrogating. Similar to the book, SPECTRE comes to the rescue in place of SMERSH doing away with Le Chiffre and his wife. However, they make sure to badly scar Bond's hand as a way of identifying him in future missions.

---

[24] This may have been inspired by the character of Valerie Mathis in the *Climax!* episode as she was working for Le Chiffre and had a pre-existing relationship with James Bond.

Unfortunately, Feldman's version of *Casino Royale* would develop into the 1967 film, a still of which is presented above.

As for Bond and Vesper, it should be noted that the duo never gets to consummate their relationship, as Vesper confesses to being a SPECTRE agent and kills herself via cyanide pill before Bond can get out of the hospital. A melancholy, grieving Bond then lays in his hospital bed, fearing that he is now impotent. However, in the last scene, Lili's girlfriend, Georgie, resurfaces to check on him. She and Bond begin to kiss, and Bond discovers that he is clearly not impotent. The end.[25]

Sadly, Hecht died not long after completing the script in mid-1964. As for Feldman, he wisely attempted to court a co-production with EON in 1964, which ultimately failed. Though it was considered for a time, Broccoli and Saltzman eventually got tired of haggling with Feldman. By then, they were used to having creative and financial control of James Bond. Besides, there were plenty of other Fleming books to adapt—back then, at least.

---

[25] Stylistically, I feel this ending fit Connery's version of the character pretty well. Also, in the interest of being thorough, the Georgie character was known as Julie in other scripts.

Undeterred, Feldman approached Sean Connery about switching sides and starring in his version. Connery agreed if Feldman would pay him $1 million, which was too hefty a price. From there, Feldman hired Irish actor Terence Cooper to play the new Bond. Over time, he also managed to attract David Niven, Ursula Andress, and Orson Welles to the project. By then, it had also turned into a spoof, and all that remained of Hecht's wonderful script was the notion of replacement 007s, which the new *Casino Royale* would run absolutely wild with.[26] When Feldman pitched his spy spoof to Columbia Pictures, they accepted, and the abomination that was the 1967 *Casino Royale* was born.

RELEASE DATE: April 1967
RUNTIME: 131 Minutes
DIRECTORS: John Huston, Ken Hughes, Val Guest, Robert Parrish & Joe McGrath
PRODUCER: Charles Feldman
SCREENPLAY: Wolf Mankowitz, John Law & Michael Sayers
MUSIC: Burt Bacharach
CAST: David Niven (Sir James Bond) Ursula Andress (Vesper Lynd/007) Peter Sellers (Evelyn Tremble/007) Orson Welles (Le Chiffre) Joanna Pettet (Mata Bond/007) Daliah Lavi (the Detainer/007) Woody Allen (Jimmy Bond)

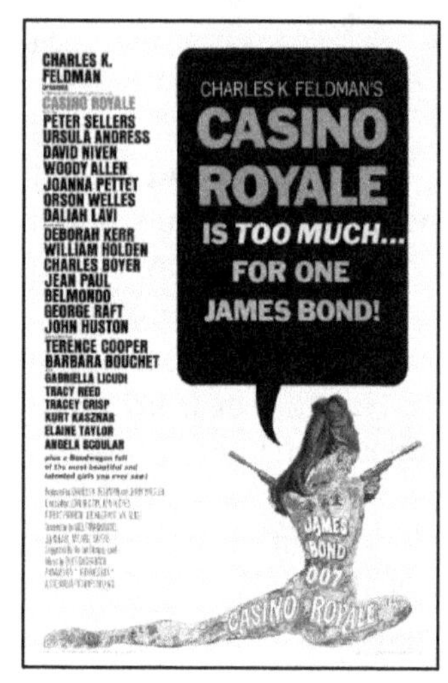

SPOOFING 007: *CASINO ROYALE* (1967)

As already stated, turning *Casino Royale* into a spoof was both a disservice to the original novel and a disastrous mistake, artistically speaking. None of the original ideas from the Hecht screenplays survived other than that a plethora of agents codenamed "James

[26] Duns, "Casino Royale: discovering the lost script," *Telegraph* (March 2, 2011).

Bond" would partake in the mission to take down Le Chiffre at Casino Royale. Joseph Heller and George Mandel worked on the new "spoof" script, which was later taken over by Billy Wilder and even more contributors, including members of the cast during shooting.

On that note, and if nothing else, 1967's *Casino Royale* boasts one of the most impressive casts of the 1960s, even if they are wasted. Headlined by David Niven and Peter Sellers, you could say this is James Bond by way of the Pink Panther franchise, just not as funny. Sellers was at the top of his game at the time, having come off of both *The Pink Panther* and its sequel, *A Shot in the Dark* (both 1964). When Sellers was approached to play James Bond, he didn't like the idea until producer Charles K. Feldman pitched it to him as a "little man playing James Bond."

Casino Royale might have been a coherent film if not for Sellers. While Sellers was shooting scenes with the character of Miss Goodthighs, offscreen, his relationship with the future Miss Goodnight and current Mrs. Sellers, Brit Ekland, was falling apart. Sellers' relationship problems bled over into production, especially in regard to Orson Welles, who had been cast as Le Chiffre. Though initially Sellers savored the notion of working with Welles, the latter found Sellers to be a prima donna. When Welles was afforded more respect than he was onset, Sellers entered a downward spiral that eventually led to him getting fired when he refused to show up to the set for several days in a row.

Filming had begun on January 11, 1966, and concluded by that same October. Initially, the film had only one director, Joe McGrath. With the original storyline now unsalvageable without Sellers, Feldman felt that perhaps the answer was to pump more stars, and with them more directors, into the project. The guest directors would all helm their own distinct segments with the new stars, like Woody Allen. How they would all fit together into a coherent narrative was something Feldman would worry about later. And, as stated earlier, with the new actors and

directors came even more rewrites to a script that was already fractured.[27] The new actors and directors also made the budget balloon out of control to the extent that the production was compared to *Cleopatra* (1963).[28]

The disjointed nature of the production and its multiple directors shows in the finished product. However, they were at least good directors, including John Huston, Ken Hughes, Val Guest, Robert Parrish, and Joe McGrath, who kicked things off.[29] Guest got the dirtiest job, that being to splice the incoherent and differing episodes together into something resembling a storyline.

And what of the final product? While the idea of a Bond film by way of *The Pink Panther* series doesn't sound bad, the exit of Sellers early on plus the addition of too many cooks in the kitchen ultimately sours and confuses the

---

[27] Peter Sellers hired his own writer, Terry Southern, to come up with new dialogue for him in hopes of upstaging Orson Welles.

[28] There is certainly some irony in the fact that Feldman felt he couldn't compete with EON's Bond productions and so turned his into a less expensive satire, provisionally at least. As the budget ballooned, Feldman may as well have tried his hand at a straightforward adaptation since *Casino Royale* ended up being more expensive than 1965's epic *Thunderball*.

[29] Vincent Canby reported for *The New York Times* what Feldman estimated each director's runtime to be with Huston coming in on the top with 38 minutes, Hughes: 25 minutes, McGrath: 20 minutes, Parrish: 20 minutes, and Guest at 26 minutes on the final segment, which was co-directed by stunt coordinator Richard Talmadge.

overall narrative. The film kicks off inauspiciously with the most rudimentary of pre-credit sequences and entails Peter Sellers introducing himself as James Bond to René Mathis—that's it. While the credit sequence that follows is well done, as is the score, the pre-credit sequence itself seems overconfident and lazy by comparison.

The film is naturally episodic due to the segmented way in which it was shot, with different actors and directors coming and going, beginning with David Niven and John Huston. Niven plays this film's version of the real James Bond, from whom all the others derived, and is called Sir James Bond. (Again, that new James Bonds replaced the original was the only concept carried over from the Hecht screenplay.) Directing and starring in the segment is Huston as M, who tries to lure Niven's older, retired Bond back into action. It should be said that the idea of Niven as a wealthy, aging 007 is a rather interesting one. However, the film has the audacity through Niven's character to berate EON's James Bond, chastising his jokey gadgets and the trail of beautiful often dead girls left in his wake. Though the film was making an attempt at self-reverential humor, it was rather pathetic considering that this *Casino Royale* didn't live up to its own potential.

After being forced out of retirement and following the death of M, Niven's Bond becomes M himself in an interesting touch. Notably, there is a nice scene of Niven returning to the old office for the first time in years and telling Miss Moneypenny that she hasn't aged a day, only

to learn that so much time has passed that it's her daughter. The rest of Niven's main episode for *Casino Royale* entails him going to a Scottish castle full of beautiful women. The sequence boasts some exploding ducks during a hunt that aren't too bad, plus a decent little car chase, but it's still not enough to elevate the film onto the level that it thinks is. After the end of the episode, Niven essentially becomes the picture's continuity thread.

The next segment is dominated by Peter Sellers and Ursula Andress, though more so the latter entails all of the existing 007 replacements in action plus the recruitment of even more. Among the multiple 007s already in existence is Andress's version of Vesper Lynd, now a secret agent herself. Therefore Andress played two different Bond girls, an honor shared only with Maud Adams, who starred in *The Man with the Golden Gun* and *Octopussy*, though Andress's distinction is a bit dubious thanks to *Casino Royale's* bad rap. Furthermore, it's doubly ironic since Andress played the first cinematic Bond girl, Honey Rider in *Dr. No*, and the first literary Bond girl, Vesper Lynd, in this picture. Andress probably fares better than any other actor in the film, both comically and otherwise. Seeing her flit around to Burt Baccarat's "The Look of Love" with Peter Sellers might not be iconic, but it's the closest thing to iconic that this film can claim.[30]

[30] Perhaps this film's biggest legacy is really *Austin Powers: International Man of Mystery*, which it had a hand in inspiring. Sellers resembles Austin Powers with his glasses, and when Sellers is being

As for Sellers, re-introduced in this segment, he is among the many new James Bond 007 recruits. His real name is Evelyn Tremble, recruited because he's a master at baccarat. However, this sequence doesn't really belong to him so much as to serve as his introduction for the casino portion with Orson Welles later. Elsewhere is also recruited a new Bond by the name of Cooper—actually Terence Cooper, the actor eyed to replace Sean Connery back when this *Casino Royale* was a straight adaptation. (Cooper is easily the best of the replacement Bonds and is trained to ignore beautiful women to counter all the dangerous female spies.)

The next replacement 007 is none other than the real James Bond's long-lost daughter, Mata Bond, the result of an affair with the real-life spy Mata Hari. Mata Bond gets one of the better portions of the film overall in terms of production value. Her segment begins with a fantastic dance number in a beautiful Indian palace, followed by her mission to East/West Berlin, which is particularly engaging from a visual standpoint. Filled with Dutch angles and unique sets, it also contains cameos from former Bond stars like Burt Kwouk, who had appeared in *Goldfinger*, and Vladek Sheybal, who had a prominent role in *From Russia with Love*.

The star segment in *Casino Royale* naturally belongs to the actual casino sequences, anchored by Sellers' 007 and Welles' Le Chiffre. As Le Chiffre is described as thick and hairy in the novel, Welles's casting was spot on for *Casino Royale,* even if the tone of this version wasn't. Welles is still wasted as Le Chiffre, though, and it's a shame we couldn't have seen him in the serious version penned by Hecht.[31]

---

photographed on the spinning bed to "The Look of Love," the inspirations of Austin Powers are particularly evident.

[31] Welles's magic tricks, which he insisted on performing (and totally out of left field), do give him a good intro in the casino scene. And, although not a part of the novel, Le Chiffre's magic tricks ironically align with the character's real-life inspiration of occultist Aleister Crowley in a way.

The exterior chosen for the casino is great, and the casino segment is intriguing to watch since it's the only portion taken directly from the novel. There's Tremble/007 and Le Chiffre playing baccarat, of course, followed by Vesper getting kidnapped, then through some messy slipshod editing, Tremble/007 is captured by Le Chiffre. The chair with the bottom cut out of it is present, though in keeping with the comedic tone, Le Chiffre simply quips to Tremble that it needs to be reupholstered. There's certainly no ball breaking and Le Chiffre tortures Tremble via psychedelic hallucinations.[32] It's also at this point that a traitorous Vesper comes along to execute Tremble, and he's out of the picture. If this was his original fate or not is hard to tell, and this was likely just the easiest point in the film to let go of Sellers.[33]

Sellers jumping ship early on necessitated altering the ending. That might be why a flying saucer enters the fray from out of nowhere to kidnap Mata Bond. (Again, since Welles's and Sellers' characters were out of the film, it lacked a proper ending.) This is where Val Guest came in and decided that David Niven should be the main continuity line of the film. Since it began with him, it would end with him, so the flying saucer lands in London to

---

[32] This actually would have been an interesting replacement for the original torture scene in a straight adaptation, which would have been too much for 1960s censors and audiences.

[33] Sellers' departure is particularly evident upon Vesper's kidnapping. For starters, an outtake of Sellers getting into a racecar to rescue Vesper had to be utilized in place of a final, proper take. Second, you don't even see Le Chiffre capture Tremble. All of a sudden, he's simply Le Chiffre's prisoner... who Vesper kills out of the blue so he can exit the picture. How much better the film would've fared had Sellers not departed early is debatable. As it was, Sellers wasn't particularly funny in the film to begin with. In the "making of" featurette, original director Joe McGrath commented that Sellers' character really didn't "add up to anything at all" and that the actor seemed "lost in the film." Some have also stated that Sellers wanted to play James Bond for real and altered his material to play it straight.

kidnap Mata, inciting daddy Bond and Miss Moneypenny to go on a rescue mission together. The trail leads right back to the casino where a surprise villain awaits: Sir James Bond's nephew and the black sheep of the family: Jimmy Bond.

Woody Allen's Jimmy Bond, who goes by the groan-inducing alias of Dr. Noah, doesn't come completely out of nowhere, as the film had at least briefly featured him earlier. Suffering from an inferiority complex, Jimmy Bond plans to release a virus that makes all women incredibly beautiful and all men shorter than he is. Actually, he has several nefarious plots up his sleeve, another of which is replacing world rulers with robot doubles. Lastly, he even has a pill that can make a man turn into an atomic bomb, which he's tricked into taking so that the movie can finally, mercifully end. The ending goes off the rails, with all kinds of nonsensical tripe from tuxedo-wearing chimps to the Frankenstein monster to cowboys and Indians storming the casino until Woody Allen explodes... And you know they don't know how to end a movie when the producers simply blow everything up, including the heroes. That's right, all the protagonists from Niven's Sir James to Miss Moneypenny die and are shown with angel wings in heaven.

Ironically, 1967's *Casino Royale* predated a few of the storylines used in the Daniel Craig era. An aging, retired Bond features heavily in *Skyfall* and *No Time to Die*. Bond being replaced by a younger female agent happened in *No Time to Die* as well, while Bond and Miss Moneypenny out in the field on a mission together occurred in *Skyfall*. Lastly, Bond reuniting with a long-lost daughter only to die at the end of the movie occurred in 1967's *Casino Royale* long before *No Time to Die*.

If nothing else, *Casino Royale* left behind an amazing poster. Actually, Orson Welles attributed much of the film's success to said poster of a naked woman tattooed with various hippie symbols. It should come as no surprise that no advance screenings were allowed as the producers knew exactly what they had on their hands. The film was originally supposed to come out during the Christmas season of 1966, but delays led to it being pushed back to April 1967. This placed it dangerously close to EON's 007 opus for 1967, *You Only Live Twice*.

As badly as *Casino Royale* might be lambasted today, it actually did make money with a healthy $41.7 million gross. However, that didn't mean that audiences liked it. Furthermore, the profit margin was still somewhat reduced considering not only the production's bloated $12 million budget, but also that star Peter Sellers had to be given a percentage of the grosses per his contract. Today, the film is probably best remembered for Burt Bacharach's Oscar-nominated song, "The Look of Love," which producer Charles Feldman ironically tried to remove from the film. On that note, Feldman died not terribly long after the stressful production finally came to an end.

DEVELOPING EON's *CASINO ROYALE*

Timing is everything as they say. While it may be tempting to say that a proper film adaptation of *Casino Royale* came too late, in foresight, just the opposite seems true. In actuality, it was a blessing in disguise that EON's *Casino Royale* took as long as it did to come to fruition. Had, for instance, EON acquired the rights to *Casino Royale* in the 1970s, it's hard to imagine Roger Moore coldly stating, "The bitch is dead now."[34] Not to mention that *Casino Royale* works exceptionally well as a James Bond origin story.

As it was, EON's *Casino Royale* came about at an opportune time for the Bond series. In the early 2000s, the franchise was at a crossroads. Not only was Pierce Brosnan tiring of playing Bond, but 2002's *Die Another Day* was borderline camp in an era that was beginning to value realism over fantasy. Comments from the producers also

[34] Connery or Dalton would have done well with the line, though.

reflect this, with 007 writer Robert Wade admitting to Screen International that "you can't go bigger than" *Die Another Day* and that 007 was in need of a reboot.

Ironically, when EON finally snared the *Casino Royale* rights, *Die Another Day* writers Neal Purvis and Robert Wade were working on a spinoff of the aforementioned film to focus on Halle Berry's character, Jinx. The duo told the website On Her Majesty's Secret Service that as they were working on it, Barbara Broccoli and Michael G. Wilson called to tell them that it was time to reread *Casino Royale*. Or, in other words, forget about Jinx and get back to James Bond.[35]

As we all know, the *Casino Royale* novel is a very grounded adventure when compared to Fleming's future works like *Goldfinger* or *Thunderball*. *Casino Royale* was perfect for the mid-2000's where Batman, not seen since the very campy, juvenile *Batman and Robin* in 1997, had successfully been rebooted in 2005's *Batman Begins*. Audiences loved it and it was a surprise financial juggernaut. As it turned out, James Bond would follow suit with a vengeance.

Even though the screenwriters and producers alike knew that Bond needed a reboot, that didn't necessarily mean doing away with Pierce Brosnan. The initial plan was more along the lines of how *For Your Eyes Only* had grounded 007 after *Moonraker*. Purvis and Wade had an interesting take on how to adapt *Casino Royale* to Brosnan's by-then-well-established portrayal of the character. (As it was, due to Brosnan's age, nor could their

---

[35] *Casino Royale* had been another casualty of a lawsuit with Ian Fleming regarding the novel *Thunderball*, which had started out as a screenplay before it was ever a book with another contributor, Kevin McClory. Because McClory helped with the overall storyline and even alleged to have dreamed up the organization of SPECTRE, McClory claimed to therefore have partial rights to SPECTRE. Of course, it's all a bit more complicated than that, but that's the simple way of explaining it and it also enabled Sean Connery's *Never Say Never Again* remake of *Thunderball* in 1983.

Casino Royale work as a prequel or origin story.) Purvis and Wade's reasoning was that Brosnan's Bond had always been quite the womanizer, and in none of the four previous outings had 007 seemed remotely serious about settling down with the leading lady.

There had been subtle hints through dialogue that Brosnan's Bond may have married Tracy or some kind of an equivalent in the past, but it was never explicitly stated as it had been in the pre-credit scene of *For Your Eyes Only* or the dialogue in *License to Kill*. Whether Brosnan's Bond had a dead wife or not, the writers' take was that no woman had ever been enticing enough for 007 to give up his license to kill. With their version of Vesper, though, Bond would be willing to permanently holster his Walther PPK by the end of the proposed film.

The film would have also dug into Bond's backstory as an orphan who never had a normal life. To get him to relate more to Vesper, Purvis and Wade were going to retcon her to be an orphan as well. As the two fall in love, Bond finally gets a taste of what true love is to the extent that, by the proposed script's end, he's ready to resign from the secret service and try his hand at a normal life with Vesper. In keeping with the novel, Vesper would still ultimately die as something of a traitor, but Bond would at least come out of his adventure able to identify with what love truly is. In that way, Bond could finally relate and identify with the normal, everyday people that he saves the world for. It was an intriguing way to turn Bond's beginning into what could've possibly been the Brosnan Bond's ending. When it was decided that Brosnan wouldn't return, rather than being discouraged, Purvis and Wade were happy to embrace the aspect of an origin story for a younger Bond.[36]

---

[36]That's where *Casino Royale's* parkour chase came in. Though Bond films had always embraced what was in vogue, which parkour certainly was in the mid-2000s, more than anything, the writers

As for other challenges in adapting *Casino Royale*, the book began with Bond already on his mission at the casino in the first chapter. As such, the screenplay lacked a first act, so Purvis and Wade decided to start things off by showing Bond's first two kills, which earned him the 00-ranking, in the pre-credits scene. They also wanted to explain how Le Chiffre found himself in hot water with his backers. Thus came the foiled terrorist plot against the airlines and the superb chase scene to go with it.[37]

Purvis and Wade also had aspirations of pulling from Fleming's previously underutilized short stories, namely "The Hildebrand Rarity" where Bond has dealings with a cruel millionaire by the name of Milton Krest and his long-suffering wife. While the character name of Milton Krest was used in *License to Kill*, the film's version was a far cry from the character of the short story. As such, the writers wanted the character of what ultimately became Alex Dimitrios in the final film to either be Milton Krest or to at least be inspired by him. In either case, Bond's friend from the short story, Fidele Barbey, was to be killed in the sequence at some point as well. At the end of the segment, Bond would aid Milton/Dimitrios's wife in stuffing a fish down his throat in order to kill him as a nod to Fleming's short story. [38]

---

wanted to showcase a younger, fleet-footed Bond engaging in a fast-paced chase on foot as opposed to the typical 007 car chases.

[37] Before that, the writers envisioned a planned hijacking of a cruise ship outside of Cape Town, South Africa, which Bond was to foil.

[38] While a nice tip of the hat to Fleming, no doubt all of the context needed to set up the death-by-fish-scene would've been difficult to establish, and removing Krest from the story probably simplified it. The duo also showed some love for what is arguably the least of the 007 stories, "007 in New York," by naming Demetrios's mistress Solange, which was a character mentioned in "007 in New York." It's the shortest of Fleming's stories and was really just an exercise in Bond's inner monologue, containing no action whatsoever. Bond is sent on a mission to New York to warn a British spy that her roommate is a double agent. Bond was supposed to rendezvous

Whereas in the book, Casino Royale was located in Royale-Les-Eaux in France, for the film, it was relocated to Montenegro because the producers felt it needed to be further removed from international banking authorities, according to the *Casino Royale* Press Kit. Likewise, Montenegro led to the end sequence set in Venice. As we all know, the book's climax hinged solely upon the doomed relationship of Bond and Vesper—there was no concluding set piece. This wouldn't fly in a film version of *Casino Royale,* which needed at least one more action sequence after the death of Le Chiffre to cap it off. Initially, Wade and Purvis envisioned some sort of horse chase through Venice until they came up with the idea of the sinking Venetian palace in the Grand Canal.[39]

However, when *Goldeneye* director Martin Campbell was hired for *Casino Royale,* he didn't care for the screenplay and asked to have Paul Haggis rewrite it to be closer to the novel. That said, and to Purvis's and Wades' credit, the duo did include the infamous torture scene, Vesper's betrayal, suicide, and even the brutal "The bitch is dead now" line. Ironically, according to Wade and Purvis, it was Campbell who changed the ending more than they did. Their version had Vesper committing suicide on her own more along the lines of the book, and then the action piece in the sinking palace would follow. Haggis and Campbell rewrote the scene to have Vesper die as a result of drowning.

The differences between Haggis's rewrite and the final screenplay are fairly minor and they can all be found in Clément Feutry's spectacular *Scripting 007* if one is curious. The only bits that I found of particular interest were some discarded choreography from the airport chase with the terrorist bomber, Carlos, entailing some additional parkour. As Bond clings to the top of the fuel

---

with her outside of the Central Park zoo's reptile house. As such, the writers wanted one of Bond's pre-credit kills to be at that location.

[39] According to director Martin Campbell, Wade and Purvis also wrote a grandiose action sequence involving a dam.

truck which is being driven by Carlos, he purposefully drives under an airplane wing in hopes of knocking off 007. Instead, Bond jumps onto the wing and dashes across it in time to jump back onto the truck. It's a great bit and it's too bad it was cut. As the chase continued, it would have greatly resembled the one from *Raiders of the Lost Ark*, with Bond being kicked through the windshield and clinging to the front bumper. With a gun he wrestled away from Carlos, Bond shoots out the tires to force a stop and eventually kills Carlos as well.

Other deleted bits of significance had Bond being airlifted by helicopter to a train station in the Swiss Alps. Upon boarding the train, he takes the place of a man named John Bliss, who was supposed to be playing in the big game. When departing the train at Montenegro, Bond would meet Vesper for the first time and engage in some clever but eventually deleted banter. Another deletion explained that Vesper was an orphan, whose father was a gambler who shot her mother and then himself.[40]

The oddest thing about this script was that it neglected Felix Leiter in place of a brand-new CIA agent to be named Grey Wolpert. The infamous torture scene initially utilized a carpet beater as in the book and also took place in an abandoned house in the country rather than the final film's barge. Unlike the novel, Vesper was to be seen seated in a chair naked as well, with Le Chiffres' mistress implying that she would torture Vesper with some pliers. Apart from an extended sequence in Venice focusing on Bond's romance with Vesper, from there, Haggis's rewrite greatly resembled the final product.

Quentin Tarantino's *Casino Royale*

Among those who greatly regretted the fact that Howard Hawks never got to direct *Casino Royale* in the 1960s was Quentin Tarantino. Although most reports said Tarantino wanted to do *Casino Royale* after *Die Another Day* with

---

[40] Perhaps it was a holdover from the old script for Brosnan's Bond?

Pierce Brosnan, he actually had ideas of doing it much sooner. In the mid-90s, after finishing *Pulp Fiction*, Tarantino reached out to the Fleming estate, keenly aware that EON still didn't have rights to *Casino Royale*. His version would've been a one-and-done affair that was stylistically separate from EON's films. However, Tarantino learned that EON had recently safeguarded *Casino Royale* so it would be impossible to produce without their permission. In 2004, after *Die Another Day's* release, Tarantino again expressed his desire to make *Casino Royale*. Although he wanted to bring back Pierce Brosnan, his *Casino Royale* would not have been in continuity with the last four EON films, set in either the 1950s or 1960s. As for other asides, it was envisioned as being shot in black and white, with Uma Thurman as Vesper Lynd and Samuel L. Jackson as Felix Leiter. Brosnan publicly voiced his support for the idea, but it was considered too risky for EON at the time, and it was never seriously considered. Still, *Casino Royale* peppered with Tarantino's always superb dialogue and presented in his distinctive style would've been quite an experience.

RELEASE DATE: November 2006
RUNTIME: 144 Minutes
DIRECTOR: Martin Campbell
PRODUCER: Michael G. Wilson & Barbara Broccoli
SCREENPLAY: Neal Purvis and Robert Wade & Paul Haggis
MUSIC: David Arnold
CAST: Daniel Craig (James Bond)
Eva Green (Vesper Lynd)
Mads Mikkelsen (Le Chiffre)
Giancarlo Giannini (René Mathis)
Jeffrey Wright (Felix Leiter)
Judi Dench (M)
Jesper Christensen (Mr. White)

WATCHING *CASINO ROYALE* (2006)

Casino Royale sets itself apart from the start with its black and white pre-credit sequence. Compared to Brosnan's past four teasers, which involved everything from freefalling into airplanes to motorboat chases on the Thames, this opener relies on Campbell's style and Craig's delivery more than anything else. As Purvis and Wade had admitted, *Die Another Day* had gone too big, and to begin this film with another whopper of an opener wouldn't have been the right move. Simply showing Bond's first two kills, one of which is brutal and the other easy and efficient, works quite well. The editing, intercutting between the hand-to-hand fight in the bathroom—Bond's first kill—and a darkened office—where Bond awaits his second—is especially effective. When Bond's second target, resigned to his fate, begins to tell him that his second kill will be easier, Craig's Bond doesn't even let him finish his statement, shooting him in the head before he can. "Yes, considerably," Bond surmises.[41]

The title sequence that follows is not only superb in its visual execution and design—based around casinos and card games—but it's the first title song sung by a male performer since 1987's *The Living Daylights,* which was also refreshing for a change. As with other Bond films in the past, it was difficult to come up with a song that matched the title of the film, and so instead, composer David Arnold came up with "You Know My Name," co-written and sung by the late Chris Cornell.

---

[41] The book doesn't feature Bond's two kills as part of the story, and are included only in the form of memories that Bond isn't terribly proud of. His first two kills, which he mentions to Mathis, are a Japanese cipher expert and a Norwegian double agent. In contrast to the film, where Bond's first kill is a difficult affair and the second is simple and straightforward, in the book, Bond's first kill goes smoothly while the second leaves a brutal, ugly mark on Bond. It's also why he considers resigning from the service at the end of the book, though, in the film, it's to tour the world with Vesper.

After a strong teaser and title sequence, *Casino Royale* doesn't lose any momentum. It keeps going strong. The parkour chase in Madagascar is the best Bond action sequence in years. The last film, *Die Another Day*, had too much overreliance on CGI and gimmicks for its set pieces. It also stretched belief as Brosnan went from driving an invisible car to windsurfing on a tidal wave, which again, was mostly all CGI and greenscreen work. It was also, in a word, bananas. As such, *Casino Royale* course corrects the series not only in its more grounded premise but also more grounded action using real performers doing actual stunts. The parkour scene is eventually followed by another stellar, heart-pounding action set piece at the Miami International Airport. Bond's cleverness in blowing up the terrorist with his own bomb is the icing on the cake to top off a scene that was fantastic to begin with. Bond's smirk at hearing the explosion is also priceless.

It's quite unusual that not only does *Casino Royale* offer its best action pieces in the first half of the film, but also that the second half doesn't falter for lack of action. By then the viewer is so invested in the new 007 that the suspenseful poker game is more than enough to hold the viewer's interest. There was also no place to put a big action scene in the casino if one were to follow the book. On that note, thankfully both the bomb blast and the cane gun from the novel are done away with and replaced with a simple poisoned martini. Upon returning to the table after his brush with death, Bond's line to Le Chiffre, "That last hand nearly killed me," is superb. Speaking of great lines, Craig said that the clincher for him was a line in the script where Bond is asked if he wants his vodka martini shaken or stirred, and he replies, "Do I look like I give a damn?" Indeed, the fact that Craig's Bond doesn't give a damn is precisely what makes him so captivating.

Bond's torture scene, naked at the mercy of Le Chiffre, is faithful to the book while also being updated with just a bit of humor. Instead of Bond yielding to the torture in any way, he eggs Le Chiffre on, taunting him that he has a "little itch" down there, then chiding Le Chiffre that he scratched his balls for him. It makes Bond look like a badass while also keeping the scene from getting too serious. The same is true in terms of how the nature of Bond's injuries are addressed. While the book explored Bond's fear of impotence after his cruel torture through his inner monologue, the film's dialogue handles the notion humorously and effectively, not being privy to inner monologues. In an exchange with Vesper, the latter tells Bond that even if all that was left of him was his pinky finger, he'd still be more of a man than anyone she'd ever met. "That's because you know what I can do with my little finger," Bond returns her heartfelt sentiment with a flirty tease.

The sinking palace along the Great Canal in Venice isn't as exciting as the preceding two big set pieces, but it also doesn't need to be. *Casino Royale* is so good that had it featured another action sequence on the level of the parkour scene or the airport chase, it would have been too much. As such, and though not as exciting as the previously mentioned action scenes, the shootout in the sinking palace is perfect. Besides, by that point, the audience is more invested in the characters than the action for once. While the book offered a pretty immersive experience in terms of Bond's final days with Vesper and her blindsiding Bond with suicide, the film's ending with Vesper taking her life in front of Bond is more impactful in the visual medium.

Casino Royale is the rare perfect film that keeps up its momentum *and* sticks its landing. Not only do we get the line "The bitch is dead now" from the book, but the final shot is ingenious. As Bond walks up to Mr. White and delivers, for the first time, his signature "Bond, James Bond" line, we cut to black and the credits roll. Some viewers were enjoying the film so much that they actually felt disappointed when the film cut off at that point. However, it was the perfect place to end it.

Casino Royale was a huge win for the Bond franchise on several fronts. Though Craig's casting as the "blonde Bond" had been contested by more than a few, audiences raved about his portrayal upon the film's release. It also course-corrected the semi-disastrous *Die Another Day* while at the same time outgrossing it by over $100 million. And though the Daniel Craig era would have its share of ups and downs overall, *Casino Royale* arguably kicked off one of the best eras the Bond franchise ever had.

LIVE AND LET DIE

PUBLICATION DATE: April 5, 1954
ORIGINAL PAGE LENGTH: 234pp.
PUBLISHER: Jonathan Cape

Some of the most memorable scenes of the James Bond franchise came from the second novel in the series, *Live and Let Die,* and yet did not appear in the 1973 film adaptation of the same name. If you are a knowledgeable fan, you'll already know this, but the bit where Bond is dragged through shark-infested waters in 1981's *For Your Eyes Only* originated in the pages of *Live and Let Die*. The same sharks that menaced Bond in the book also made an amputee out of Felix Leiter. That's right; although the dramatic scene of Leiter being lowered into a shark tank in 1989's *License to Kill* fit the film's darker atmosphere to a tee, it, too, originated in Fleming's second James Bond outing.[42]

[42] Therefore, in all the Bond books to follow, Felix Leiter appeared as an amputee with a hook-hand.

As for my own take on the *Live and Let Die* film, I realized at a young age that the Bond movies tended to utilize themes and motifs—I would not call them gimmicks—to flavor each entry and to set them apart. It was evident to me that *Thunderball* was defined by its underwater sequences while the same was true of *Moonraker* for its outer space scenes. Other Bond films were defined by their locations, Las Vegas in the case of *Diamonds Are Forever* and Japan in *You Only Live Twice*. As a teenager who had loved *Shaft*, I simply assumed that *Live and Let Die* was cooked up by the producers to be a James Bond-Blaxploitation movie. And while I wasn't necessarily wrong in that assumption, I also had no idea that the film was based on one of the earliest James Bond novels.

For those only familiar with the 1973 film, the novel features the same general storyline of James Bond going up against a group of black villains, led by the mysterious Mr. Big, who utilizes voodoo as a means of control and intimidation. However, in the book's case, Mr. Big is also a SMERSH operative who uses the lost treasure of Sir Henry Morgan to finance his operations. While the psychic love interest Solitaire is the female lead, there are no Tarot cards or smuggled drugs at play, nor are there crocodile farms or mechanical-armed henchmen, that would come later.

WRITING *LIVE AND LET DIE*

Ian Fleming was wisely advised by a fellow novelist, Michael Arlen, to begin work on Bond #2 before the first reviews for *Casino Royale* could come in. Knowing from experience, Arlen warned Fleming that as good as *Casino Royale* was, any bad reviews might take the heart out of him, thus lessening his inspiration for the sequel. Fleming took the words of Arlen to heart and finished *Casino Royale's* sequel before it was published and could be reviewed.

As it turned out, the writing process for *Live and Let Die* established a creative process/pattern that Fleming would follow for many years. Specifically, in the winter months of the new year, Fleming would research and flesh out a novel at his Goldeneye home in Jamaica. During the middle of the year, he would address editorial points from his publishers, make revisions, and would review the final proofs for publication by the end of the year. Over the course of that same year, he would inevitably also be developing the sequel consciously and subconsciously, oftentimes during his own real-life adventures.

Case in point, in preparing to write *Live and Let Die*, in early 1953, Fleming traveled to St. Petersburg, Florida, to inspect a live worm factory. Prior to that, in December of 1952, Fleming had visited the nightclubs of Harlem. Aside from going scuba diving for lost Spanish doubloons on his own, Fleming initially settled for simply consulting with Spink, London's leading experts on coins. Ironically though, in April of 1953, a *Sunday Times* assignment enabled Fleming to travel to France to go diving with Jock Cousteau. Fitting with his burgeoning novel, and as Fleming's luck would have it, Cousteau was investigating a Greek galleon that had sunk off the coast of an island near Marseilles. Although Fleming actually diving with Cousteau was not a stipulation from the *Sunday Times*, Fleming, who had scuba diving experience, convinced Cousteau to let him tag along to the galleon. And thus, Fleming garnered first-hand experience for his underwater sequences where Bond swims into a cave where the lost treasure is stored.

Initially, Fleming called the book "The Undertaker's Wind" in reference to a death-bringing wind meant to be an analogy for Bond himself. It stemmed from a scene where Bond's guide and boat captain, Quarrel, explained Jamaican folklore to Bond, specifically that the nighttime breeze, the "Undertaker's Wind," blew the bad air out of the islands before being replaced by the "Doctor's Wind" in the morning, which brought the good wind in.

Though not a bad title, Fleming relegated it to a chapter header instead and named the book after a bit of clever dialogue spoken by Bond, which interestingly was not carried over into the film. (During a meeting between Bond and a U.S. agent, the latter says that it's their policy to "live and let live" where Mr. Big is concerned. Bond replies, "In my job, when I come up against a man like [Mr. Big], I have another motto. It's 'live and let die.'")

Live and Let Die received not only rave reviews from beta readers who gave Fleming his first dose of feedback, but also upon its official publication. Its initial print run of 7,500 copies in Great Britain swiftly sold out, necessitating a second printing that same year.

READING *LIVE AND LET DIE*

Perhaps knowing that a briefing in M's office was a bland way to start the book, Fleming reintroduces us to James Bond as he makes his landing at a New York airport, followed by a flashback to M's office so that we know just what Bond's mission is. His assignment is to investigate the crime lord known as Mr. Big, suspected of selling Sir Henry Morgan's lost gold coins to help finance SMERSH operations in the United States.

In New York, Bond reunites with an old pal from *Casino Royale*, CIA agent Felix Leiter, and the duo take a trip to the nightclubs of Harlem. Both are captured, and while Leiter is taken away to be beaten by Mr. Big's henchmen, Bond gets an audience with the big man himself along with the beautiful Solitaire, Mr. Big's captive psychic. Bond's first meeting with Mr. Big sports some fantastic dialogue. Although the core of the scene made it into the film version, some great Fleming dialogue for Mr. Big went unutilized. For instance, Mr. Big tells Bond he has what the ancient Christians called "accidie," a "deadly lethargy" that enveloped those who had sated all of their desires. "I have, literally, no more worlds to conquer in my chosen orbit," he laments. As such, he chooses to be an absolute master at his craft. Mr. Big, knowing the prejudices of the time, basically explains to Bond that since he can't acquire any more power in the realm of international crime rings due to his race, he strives for absolute perfection in his operations.

Bond's meeting with Mr. Big is quasi-similar to the film version. Instead of threatening to cut off Bond's finger, Tee-Hee, who doesn't have mechanical hands with snippers, threatens to break Bond's finger. And, unlike the movie, Tee-Hee follows through on his threat, snapping Bond's finger, creating an injury that inhibits Bond for the rest of the book. As for Solitaire, also introduced in this scene, while she is psychic, she doesn't rely on Tarot cards. Instead, a usual deck of cards serves her intuition.[43]

The sequence concludes with Bond getting the better of Tee-Hee by escaping and reuniting with Leiter, who was purposefully let go. Later, Bond receives a surprise visit from Solitaire, who begs Bond to rescue her from Mr. Big, which he obliges.[44] This leads to a sequence of Bond and Solitaire taking the train from New York to Florida. Unlike the film, the duo isn't menaced by Tee-Hee, who Bond has already dispatched. Instead, sensing danger, the duo gets off the train before an assassination attempt occurs, off-page, where their car is attacked.

In Florida, Bond reunites with Leiter to investigate a worm factory/aquarium owned by Mr. Big and named

---

[43] Although Fleming was always well-researched, I can't help but wonder if Solitaire not using Tarot cards in the book was an oversight on his part.

[44] By contrast, in the film, it's Bond who goes to Solitaire and induces her to run away.

after the mythical Ouroboros. Said worm factory also has a shark tank, which Leiter finds himself lowered into around the same time that Solitaire gets kidnapped, giving Bond a double whammy. Leiter survives minus a limb, and Bond sets off for Jamaica, where he is matched with a Jamaican boat captain named Quarrel, who sails him to Mr. Big's island.[45] Off the coast of the island, Bond goes scuba diving and plants a mine on Mr. Big's yacht undetected. However, a scuffle with some barracuda necessitates that Bond make a quick escape. Unable to get back to Quarrel's boat, he swims into an underwater cavern and right into Sir Henry Morgan's treasure cave, which also happens to be Mr. Big's lair. There, Bond is reunited with Solitaire and recaptured by Mr. Big, who spouts off some more great dialogue that went unutilized in the film. (Upon their reunion, Mr. Big tells Bond, "The fly has indeed been a long time coming to the spider, or perhaps I should say the minnow to the whale.")

This all leads into the iconic scene of Mr. Big towing a bound Bond and Solitaire behind his yacht through the shark and barracuda-inhabited waters. As stated before, this sequence didn't make it into the *Live and Let Die* film and was transplanted into 1981's *For Your Eyes Only*. Reading the scene vs. watching it in the aforementioned film is certainly interesting, with one being privy to Bond's thoughts. (Notably, Bond contemplates drowning Solitaire as a way of sparing her the decidedly more traumatic death of being eaten by sharks.) This method of execution also ties in nicely with the Sir Henry Morgan subplot, as Mr. Big states that Morgan used to execute prisoners in the same manner.

Unlike in *For Your Eyes Only*, where Bond must devise an escape, in the book, Bond merely has to wait out the timed

---

[45] In the film adaptation of *Live and Let Die*, Bond sails with Quarrel Jr. due to the fact that Quarrel had died in the *Dr. No* movie. So, it's interesting to note that in the books, Quarrel appears first in *Live and Let Die* and returns for *Dr. No*, the 6th book in the series.

explosion of the mine he placed on Mr. Big's yacht earlier. Bond and Solitaire manage to avoid the toothy fish, the yacht explodes, and Bond watches as Mr. Big is pulled under by one of the sharks. After that, Quarrel comes to their rescue, and Bond and Solitaire go off to lick their respective wounds, so to speak, on an island paradise.

For many, the highlights of the book probably comprise the climatic portion just summarized along with a shootout in the aquarium full of poisonous fish.[46] But for me, it was in Bond's interactions with Mr. Big where the writing proved especially captivating via the dialogue. Also of note is Bond's relationship with Felix Leiter, which one might argue forms the book's emotional core. While Bond has a healthy affection for Solitaire, I would guess Fleming didn't want Bond falling in love again as he did with Vesper in the previous book. As such, the third act is primarily driven by the maiming of Felix Leiter. Yes, Bond is out to save Solitaire, too, but more than anything, he's enraged by the cruel fate of his friend. Notably, and unlike in *License to Kill*, Leiter's dip in the shark tank happens off-page, so to speak. I would guess this was because Fleming didn't like to break from Bond's perspective, and that way the reader could experience Bond's own shock at discovering Leiter's bloody body in his hotel room.

Ultimately, *Live and Let Die* stands as a worthy follow-up to *Casino Royale*. Fleming did an excellent job of retaining Bond's essence while at the same time not repeating the previous entry by placing his hero in entirely different settings, spanning the nightclubs of Harlem to the seafloor of Jamaica. Fleming especially excelled with his characters, providing interesting villains and a unique female lead while also building on the relationship between Bond and Leiter. The novel also has quite a legacy regarding the film franchise, since elements of *Live and Let Die* were utilized in several different Bond films.

---

[46] Bond's stroll along the sea floor, where he tussles with an octopus and escapes some barracuda, was also quite exciting.

DEVELOPING EON's *LIVE AND LET DIE*

Film rights for *Live and Let Die* were optioned right out of the gate. Whether it was due to the television adaptation of *Casino Royale* or simply the *Live and Let Die* novel itself, Warner Bros offered a rather paltry $500 option on *Live and Let Die*, with another $5,000 to follow if they made the film. Thankfully, Fleming turned them down, finding the sum too low. Had he accepted, and Warner Bros bungled the film, James Bond may not have survived into modern times.

It's interesting that despite being the second Bond book, it was the eighth film in the series. Perhaps the *Thunderball* film, with its tropical settings and underwater photography, made Broccoli and Saltzman wary of being repetitive considering the *Live and Let Die* novel featured tropical settings and underwater scenes as well. Nor was it the producers who decided it was time to adapt *Live and Let Die* in lieu of the success of movies like *Shaft* and the Blaxploitation genre. It was actually screenwriter Tom Mankiewicz who made the decision.

Broccoli had given Mankiewicz several books to choose from, including *Moonraker*, but Mankiewicz gravitated towards *Live and Let Die* due to Mr. Big and the villains. Keenly aware of the changing times, both in cinema and the real world, Mankiewicz felt *Live and Let Die* was the one to go with. "I wanted to do *Live and Let Die* because I thought it had more of an edge to it. Because all the villains were black and I knew it was very chancy thing because we were making it in the time of the Black Panthers, we were making it in the time of, really, a black revolution," Mankiewicz said.[47]

However, Mankiewicz felt the Cold War angle, specifically Mr. Big as a SMERSH operative, was by now outdated. To make the film more topical, Mankiewicz decided to utilize the current drug problem in America as the main threat as opposed to nuclear warheads and laser-

[47] Cork, *Inside Live and Let Die*, (1999).

shooting satellites. Thus, drugs replaced sunken treasure and the idea of Mr. Big working with the Soviets was dropped altogether.[48] Mankiewicz's first treatment, completed in May 1972, had a similar ending to the book, with Bond and Solitaire being dragged behind Mr. Big's yacht. That climax followed over into draft number two with one difference, that being that Mr. Big was no longer eaten by his own sharks as in the book. Instead, Mankiewicz preferred the idea of Bond shooting Mr. Big with an anti-shark gun that makes him inflate and then explode.

The famous crocodile scene was invented while scouting locations in Jamaica when the producers came across a sign reading "Trespassers will be eaten." Originally, instead of a crocodile farm, Mr. Big owned either a coffee plantation or a sugar factory where Bond would face peril in the form of a gigantic granulator. An even worse scenario envisioned Bond tossed into a giant dryer – an idea that Mankiewicz pointed out was Saltzman's, not his. Lastly, the trip to the crocodile farm also resulted in renaming the villain Ross Kananga, after the owner of the farm.

While Jamaica served as a major location in the book, New Orleans did not. As covered earlier, Bond's American portion of the book was split between Harlem and Florida. Florida was switched for New Orleans due to returning series director Guy Hamilton being a huge jazz fan. (That, and Florida had already featured as a major location in Hamilton's *Goldfinger*.) With the Louisiana setting came the idea for the bayou boat chase, which emerged as the most memorable action sequence of the film. That said, the boat chase was also a holdover from an old *Diamonds Are Forever* script that concluded with a boat chase on Lake Mead.

---

[48] Richard Maibaum, the series writer for many past 007 scripts, criticized the plot in a 1983 *Starlog* interview, stating that "to process drugs in the middle of the jungle is not a Bond caper."

Speaking of *Diamonds Are Forever*, initially *Live and Let Die* was still envisioned for Sean Connery—or perhaps it was just written for Connery out of habit. Notably, Saltzman had an idea he wanted to see play out with Connery. He was so excited by it that Mankiewicz remembered Saltzman calling him in the middle of the night and telling him, "Here's the scene. Sean's asleep. He thinks he's in bed with Solitaire. He feels something, wakes up, and there's a crocodile in bed with him. Isn't that great?"[49] No crocodile ever sneaks into Bond's bed, although a snake does slip into his bathtub.[50] Nor was Connery interested in returning as his salary for *Diamonds Are Forever* had been enough to meet his financial needs.

With producers having settled on Roger Moore as the new James Bond, just as they had done with George Lazenby in *On Her Majesty's Secret Service*, they wanted to be sure that the script reflected that this was the same James Bond. Or, that was to say that Moore's Bond had been on the same adventures as Connery's and shared the same continuity. To this end, it was briefly considered to have Ursula Andress reprise her role as Honey Rider from *Dr. No*. Since Honey Rider was from Jamaica, it wouldn't have been totally out of left field for her to appear. The specifics of her role have never been revealed other than Mankiewicz simply mentioning they toyed with the notion. Perhaps she would've taken the place of Quarrel Jr. as the captain of the boat?

On that note, Quarrel Jr. served as the continuity tie between Moore's Bond and Connery's. In the original script, Bond was to say to Rosie Carver regarding Quarrel Jr. that "His father and I locked horns with a Doctor named No several years ago."[51] The original boat scene with Quarrel Jr. also introduced the idea of the exploding shark

---

[49] Mankiewicz, *My Life as a Mankiewicz*, p.147.

[50] Oddly, in the first draft, Bond incapacitates the snake by headbutting it! After that, he decapitates it with his mirror.

[51] Feutry, *Scripting 007*, p.503.

bullets that figured into the climax. As it was, the exploding shark bullet used on Mr. Big was introduced late in the film. Mankiewicz placing it earlier in the script perhaps would have served as a more appropriate and natural way of foreshadowing the villain's demise.[52] It also gave a great quip for Bond, who, upon seeing an exploding shark, says something along the lines of, "Wait until Q hears about this."[53]

Ahead of his time, initially Mankiewicz race swapped Solitaire, making her black (in the book she's white). This would have at once made the Bond series more inclusive and would also have offset the black villains by having the female hero be black also.[54] Mankiewicz had the ingenious idea to hopefully cast Diana Ross, who could by default also sing the title song, creating great publicity. However, United Artists was fearful that distributors in other countries would not allow for an interracial romance and dictated that Solitaire revert to being white as in the book. A more valid and flattering reason for not

Advance poster featuring Roger Moore.

[52] Kananga testing the bullet on a couch that Whisper sits upon in the finished film is admittedly humorous, though.

[53] Q did not appear in the early scripts, either, for those no doubt wondering. Desmond Llewelyn was not unavailable, by the way, and in the actor's opinion, Saltzman wanted a break from all the gadgets... except the exploding shark bullets and magnetic watch.

[54] Quarrel and Strutter are technically the only black characters on Bond's side since Rosie turns out to be a double-agent.

using Diana Ross was that she would potentially overshadow the new James Bond, Roger Moore. Had Connery returned, this would not have been as much of an issue, but with Moore just settling into the role, it was feared that it would be Ross's movie as opposed to Moore's. (Whether or not Diana Ross was ever even asked is unknown.)

One of the bigger changes made by Mankiewicz and the producers was in regard to Mr. Big/Dr. Kananga. It should be clarified that in the book there is no Dr. Kananga, only Mr. Big, whose name comes not only from his size, but also his initials: Buonaparte Ignace Gallia. In the book, due to a heart condition, Mr. Big's skin has turned ashen grey, and combined with his bulk makes him somewhat Frankenstein-like. This detail was important to the book because it made the more superstitious-minded believe that Mr. Big was a zombie. And not just any zombie, but the personal zombie of Baron Samedi, thus making him synonymous with Baron Samedi, a real figure in voodoo belief. As we all know, the film chose to make Baron Samedi a flesh and blood character. However, the film is vague as to whether or not Baron Samedi is a folk performer or a real supernatural entity.[55]

Essentially, the film adaptation split Mr. Big into three different characters. There's Dr. Kananga, the refined dignitary, Baron Samedi, the boogeyman who keeps locals at bay, and finally, Mr. Big, the American crime lord—really just Dr. Kananga in disguise. In that sense, the Mr. Big of the book appears with a twist in that he's a ruse. It was probably for the best that the producers tailored the character to actor Yaphet Kotto, though, who arguably played one of the better villains of the franchise.

Some of Mankiewicz's other deviations were also improvements over the novel. Although it makes sense for

[55] Considering he shows up alive and well in the final shot after having died, the film's Baron Samedi is either an actual supernatural entity, or one hell of a magician.

Solitaire to play the card game of the same name, which she does in the book, considering the supernatural element of the story, it made just as much sense to have Solitaire use Tarot cards. The film upped the supernatural ante in other ways, too. While the literary Mr. Big simply used loudspeakers of voodoo drums to frighten locals away from his island, Dr. Kananga uses real voodoo practitioners led by Baron Samedi. And while the movie may have axed the yacht scene, it did retain the villain's pet sharks. As in the book, the villain's main lair is a cave, though the movie version naturally embellished it.

As to other upgrades made to the film, it was by then a must for the villain to have some kind of unique henchman à la Oddjob. While the book did include the character of Tee-Hee, he was simply Mr. Big's muscle, and nothing special at that. In fact, he was dispatched by Bond in Harlem early on and not seen again. The idea to make Tee-Hee an amputee with a metal arm fits well with the crocodile farm, his reason for missing the arm, and also to make him unique in general. Tee-Hee also provides the film with a nice action capper.

Beginning with *Goldfinger*, the Bond films started an irregular tradition where, occasionally, one of the villains would pop up again at the very end to give Bond one last row. The previous film had seen Connery's 007 dispatch Mr. Wint and Mr. Kidd, and this one had Tee-Hee popping up on the train to attack Bond and Solitaire. This, too, came from the book in a roundabout way, where Bond and Solitaire took a train bound for Florida. While Tee-Hee didn't attack the duo in the book, as he was already dead, Mankiewicz inserting him into the last scene set on the train car was certainly an interesting deviation.

These, of course, are only but a few of the many differences between the early scripts and the final version, which you can read about in depth in the excellent *Scripting 007* book by Clément Feutry.

JOHN LEMAY

RELEASE DATE: June 27, 1973
RUNTIME: 121 Minutes
DIRECTOR: Guy Hamilton PRODUCERS: Albert R. Broccoli & Harry Saltzman
SCREENPLAY: Tom Mankiewicz
MUSIC: George Martin
CAST: Roger Moore (James Bond) Yaphet Kotto (Dr. Kananga/ Mr. Big) Jane Seymour (Solitaire) Julius W. Harris (Tee-Hee) Geoffrey Holder (Baron Samedi) David Hedison (Felix Leiter) Gloria Hendry (Rosie Carver) Roy Stewart (Quarrel Jr.) Clifton James (Sheriff J.W. Pepper) Bernard Lee (M) Lois Maxwell (Moneypenny)

WATCHING *LIVE AND LET DIE* (1973)

For many fans, *Live and Let Die* has two major offenses as a Bond film. It lacks Q and also the exciting pre-credit sequence that had by then become an expected staple of the series. Instead, Moore's Bond gets a rather inauspicious post-credit introduction being awakened in bed with a beautiful woman. While the scene offers a rare glimpse of Bond's home, it runs the risk of making Bond lose some of his mystique in the process. Lack of a typical pre-title sequence aside, the rest of the action is superb, the two standouts being the crocodile farm escape and the bayou boat chase. Both sequences are clever and creative. And in a world dominated by CGI—and understandably to not endanger human lives in stunt work—Bond's dash across the live crocodiles is all the more thrilling today. (Well, not Bond, but Ross Kananga, the owner of the crocodile farm.)

In my book, a good action piece needs to be either immensely suspenseful or incredibly fun. The brief flit across the crocodiles presents the former, and the boat chase is definitely the latter. While there's not a great deal of suspense, as Bond always seems to have the upper hand during the chase, it's undeniably fun. It's further lightened by the presence of Sheriff J.W. Pepper, a love him or hate him "good ol' boy" sheriff played exclusively for laughs. (For audiences of the time, it was the former, as he was popular enough to get a reprisal in the next outing.)

Another fun, minor action sequence features Bond commandeering a passenger plane at the airport. The idea was that of Guy Hamilton, who found the concept of an airplane chase where the airplane never leaves the ground to be quite funny and ironic—and it is. It's made all the better by Bond's "copilot," Mrs. Bell. The capper of the finished scene with Bond quipping, "Same time tomorrow, Mrs. Bell?" couldn't be better.

The voodoo sequences that bookend the film coincided with an occult horror boom that would kick off later that year with the release of *The Exorcist*. Seeing James Bond crossing swords with the supernatural—he gets into a machete fight with a seemingly invincible Baron Samedi—was certainly interesting. And while on the one hand, it seemed an unforgivable sin to deprive audiences of Fleming's wonderful yacht scene that concluded the book, at the same time, Dr. Kananga's death via exploding shark bullet is certainly unique. Nor is Bond's tussle with Kanaga the last action piece of the picture. The film almost makes up for its lack of an exciting pre-credit scene with its end capper on the train, arguably the best one since *Goldfinger*.

Speaking of *Goldfinger*, this is one of Guy Hamilton's better Bonds considering his other two efforts comprised *Diamonds Are Forever* and *The Man with the Golden Gun*. Hamilton did especially well directing the pivotal scene where Dr. Kananga learns that Solitaire slept with Bond and has therefore lost her powers. Hamilton's direction, along with the actors' performances, plus the score by George Martin, make for a truly tense sequence that reaches an excellent crescendo by its conclusion.

Hamilton also had the challenge of introducing a new Bond actor in something of a fish-out-of-water scenario at that. In that regard, he and Roger Moore both succeed against the odds. For the most part, Moore plays it somewhat safe in his first outing compared to his later efforts. He's not out to make you smirk at every turn as in future entries, and a scene where he threatens Rosie Carver is more akin to Connery's Bond. He also manipulates Solitaire into bed via a Tarot card deck stacked in his favor. Those scenes aside, Moore presented a somewhat warmer, more charming Bond than Connery did, making the character his own.

Of course, Bond is only as good as his opponent, and the villains of *Live and Let Die* offer an embarrassment of riches. Most Bond films have only one distinct henchman like Oddjob. This one has the pincher-handed Tee-Hee and the supernatural Baron Samedi. Even Whisper, the quiet, not-so-gentle giant, isn't half bad as a unique henchman. Furthermore, you also get two main villains for the price of one since Dr. Kananga doubles as Mr. Big in makeup. Yaphet Kotto is positively superb as Dr. Kananga, and even if his casting meant changing the character of Mr. Big, it was worth it to see Kotto play the heavy. Although some have taken the film to task for the fact that the villains were all people of color, Kotto's Kananga never becomes a caricature and presents a charming but deadly villain that is arguably better than Charles Gray's Blofeld from the previous entry.

The film was a resounding financial success, surprisingly outgrossing Connery's *Diamonds Are Forever* despite featuring a new, untested James Bond. It also presented one of the more unique entries of the series in the sense that it's both a supernatural Bond film and something of a Blaxploitation movie in its own right.

Live and Let Die in *License to Kill*

1989's *License to Kill*, originally titled *License Revoked*, was the first Bond film not titled after or based upon an Ian Fleming story or book. While it did lift one character name from "The Hildebrand Rarity," I would argue that the main basis for the film was a sequence from *Live and Let Die*, that being the maiming of Felix Leiter. In a touch of

irony, *Live and Let Die's* David Hedison reprised Leiter for *License to Kill,* and thus Hedison's iteration of the character got to take Leiter's fateful dip in the shark tank that he should have endured in *Live and Let Die*. Whereas in the *Live and Let Die* novel, Leiter's cruel maiming drove the third act and took place off-page, in *License to Kill,* it drives the entire story, occurring on film in the first act. As in the book, Bond finds a bloodied Leiter with the note reading, "He disagreed with something that ate him."

Live and Let Die is arguably the Bond bromance book, in our modern parlance, and the same is true of the first act of *License to Kill*. The whole pre-credit scene showcases the friendship between Bond and Leiter. Robert Davi's Sanchez has similarities to both Mr. Big of the *Live and Let Die* book and Kananga of the film. Like Mr. Big, he's essentially a gangster/drug dealer who holds extra power due to his possession of surface-to-air Stinger missiles. Like Kananga, he also boasts a great deal of political power, albeit behind the scenes, of the fictional Republic of Isthmus. And, though she's not psychic like Solitaire, nor the primary Bond girl, Talisa Soto's Lupe Lamora is a captive lover not unlike Solitaire in need of rescuing.[56]

Bond's trip to Milton Krest's aquarium in *License to Kill* was probably inspired by Bond's midnight raid on the Ouroboros worm factory/aquarium owned by Mr. Big in *Live and Let Die*. The shotgun-touting manager of the aquarium in the book is nearly as slimy as Anthony Zerbe's

---

[56] Yes, I know Solitaire wasn't Mr. Big's lover, but he had plans of one day making her his lover in both the book and the film.

Krest in *License to Kill*. In *Live and Let Die*, Bond digs into a tank of poisonous fish to find Henry Morgan's gold, whereas in *License to Kill,* he finds bags of cocaine concealed underneath a tray of sea maggots. The fight in the aquarium in the *Live and Let Die* novel features exploding fish tanks that rain down poisonous fish and ends with the aquarium manager being fed to a shark. Actually, it's probably important to note that Leiter was maimed in the Ouroboros worm factory, just as he's maimed in Krest's aquarium in *License to Kill*. And like the aquarium manager fed to his own shark, Bond feeds the dirty DEA agent who sold out Leiter, Ed Killifer, to the same sharks. So, I'll stick to my theory that the action scene in the aquarium was inspired by the one in the *Live and Let Die* book.

MOONRAKER

PUBLICATION DATE: April 5, 1955
ORIGINAL PAGE LENGTH: 256pp.
PUBLISHER: Jonathan Cape

I first saw the *Moonraker* movie at the age of ten—the perfect age to see it. As such, I hold it in a little higher esteem than many other Bond fans. Heck, for a while it might've been my favorite 007 film. You've got Jaws pushing Bond out of a plane without a parachute, speed boat chases on the Amazon River, and Bond making it into outer space without the whole thing collapsing under its own insane weight. What's not to love for a ten-year-old?

Today, I still quite enjoy *Moonraker*. Though, I have to admit, had I seen it as an adult weaned on *From Russia with Love* or, more recently, the Daniel Craig films, I'm not sure how I would take *Moonraker*. During a first-time viewing, the film moves too quickly to question its logic. But if you've seen it half a dozen times, just how ludicrous it all is becomes very apparent. Case in point, as an adult, I realize that the locations picked for the film were chosen simply because they were cool. Drax could have built his hidden launch base somewhere inconspicuous, but because Cubby Broccoli had seen Iguazu Falls on a publicity tour for *The Spy Who Loved Me*, Drax's base ended up in South America in a hollowed-out Mayan temple.[57] The same was true of Bond going to the special glass factory in Venice. Drax's factory could have been anywhere, but Venice had canals, and canals allowed for the famous gondola chase, and you get the idea.

I was quite surprised when I learned just how different the book was from the film. I always assumed that Bond made it into space in the book as well. It was, after all, called *Moonraker*. I was further surprised to learn that it predated many of the other James Bond adaptations, as it was only the third book in the series. And for the last, perhaps greatest surprise, was that *Moonraker* was actually the first planned Bond film per Ian Fleming.

WRITING *MOONRAKER*

What had planted the seed for Bond to become a big screen property in Ian Fleming's mind was a letter from British film producer Alexander Korda stating how much he enjoyed *Live and Let Die* in 1954. Although Korda wasn't looking to adapt *Live and Let Die*, he did ask Fleming if he would be interested in writing screenplays. Fleming responded that, coincidentally, his next James Bond novel was "an expansion of a film story" he'd "had in my mind since the war" and "a straight thriller with particularly English but also general appeal, and involving the destruction of London by a super V.2, allowing for some wonderful film settings..."[58]

The idea of James Bond #3 being a film seemed to inhibit rather than enhance Fleming's writing process, though. If anything, it seemed that the idea put too much pressure on him. As it was, Korda felt that screenplays written as

[57] I halfway suspected that was the case, because even I fall prey to making my novels work around "cool settings" that really make no sense. But, if Cubby did it, then I guess I'm not so bad.

[58] Fleming, *Man with the Golden Typewriter*, p.54.

screenplays worked best for films, as opposed to books adapted into screenplays. Therefore, Fleming was determined to give his third Bond adventure a cinematic pace as he turned his old treatment into a full-length novel.[59]

Moonraker didn't require much traveling for research, considering that most of the story's action was confined to Kent County in England. (This, I wonder, if Fleming did as a way of keeping a potential film's budget down.[60]) Most of Fleming's research was "armchair research," unusual for him. For matters pertaining to rocketry, Fleming consulted with the British Interplanetary Society. Fleming also researched the traits of megalomaniacs to build the character of Drax, visiting Wimpole Street psychiatrist Eric Strauss. It was Strauss who pointed Fleming to the book *Men of Genius*, which gave Fleming the idea to give Drax diastema, a gap between the two front teeth as a result of constant childhood thumb-sucking, apparently a trait of megalomaniacs in many cases.

The title of the book also proved to be somewhat problematic. When he was visited by his friend, fellow author and actor Noël Coward, Fleming told him about his book, then called "The Moonraker."[61] Coward reminded Fleming that a book with that title already existed. Fleming and his publishers would eventually settle simply on *Moonraker* at the suggestion of Wren Howard, but before that, Fleming considered a menagerie of replacements. Among them were "The Moonraker Secret," "The Moonraker Plot," "Bond & the Moonraker," "The Moonraker Scare" and "The Moonraker Plan." Titles to exclude *Moonraker* altogether included "The Inhuman

---

[59] When it was too short to make for a full-length novel, Fleming then added in the scenes of Bond and Drax playing bridge.

[60] Strange though that might sound today, one has to remember *Dr. No* nor its sequels had been adapted yet.

[61] Fleming would later want Coward to portray the titular *Dr. No* in 1962, which Coward turned down.

Element," "Wide of the Mark," "The Infernal Machine," "Out of the Clear Sky" and "Mondays are Hell."

Moonraker was another success when released in 1955, although some readers were somewhat bored by Bond sticking to England, as they were accustomed to the first 007 adventures' exotic locations.

READING *MOONRAKER*

Moonraker is a bit of an odd outing for Bond in that it sticks to England, 007 doesn't get the girl and doesn't save the day in a neat, tidy fashion. Although Bond does save London, in rerouting the Moonraker missile, 200 innocents are still killed. But I'm getting ahead of myself.

The book's original title, "Mondays Are Hell," derives from the fact that the book begins on a Monday, with Bond referencing the aborted title early in the book.[62] To that end, the story is divided into sections by days of the week, concluding on Friday. *Moonraker* is kicked off rather innocuously by M wanting Bond to get to the bottom of Hugo Drax cheating at cards—hardly a herald of the apocalypse. As it is, M plays bridge with Drax at a high-end gentleman's club, The Blades, and suspects that Drax cheats despite being one of the richest men in the country. Not only is Drax mega-rich, he's mega-powerful as the

[62] The first few chapters offer a nice peak into Bond's everyday life including the mundane office work he does when he's not on missions, and even gives the name of his housekeeper, May.

money behind the Moonraker project, a super rocket that will serve as a defense and nuclear deterrent for England. As to why Drax's cheating habits are of any consequence to M, it's because Drax has become a national hero. Therefore, M fears that the scandal could permanently sour the Moonraker, which has become paramount to national defense. Rather than exposing Drax, it's M's hope that Bond can scare the millionaire straight.

The resulting sequence has the novelty of Bond and M on a sort of mission together, something the films wouldn't try until *Skyfall*. It also presents an excellent introduction to Drax, an obnoxious, disfigured braggart who is quite different from Michael Lonsdale's more refined version of the character in the film. (The only thing that the film Drax and the character of the novel have in common is that both are ultra rich.) Eventually, it's revealed that Drax isn't an English patriot but an undercover Nazi thirsting for revenge on England. To that end, the Moonraker's test launch is no such thing. Its true purpose is to obliterate London in an atomic blast. And it all would have gone to plan had M not noticed Drax cheating at cards... Or maybe not.

While the bridge sequence between Bond and Drax allowed Fleming to show his finesse once again at writing engaging card scenes and to give Bond and Drax a good sparring session, it wasn't crucial to the story. Per Fleming's own admission, the bridge sequence was never present in the film treatment that spawned the book, and he only added the scene to make it "book-length," as they say. In some ways it shows, because the rubber doesn't really meet the road until a murder occurs at Drax's Moonraker installation, necessitating that Bond go investigate.[63]

[63] Beta readers for the book concurred that it got off to a slow start, but then took off at light speed later. Humorously, one beta reader warned Fleming that Bond and M came across as Holmes and Watson during the bridge scene. [Fleming, *Golden Typewriter*, p.60.]

This results in Bond teaming with the female lead, Gala Brand, a policewoman from Scotland Yard working as Drax's secretary. Other than being an undercover female agent in Drax's employ, Gala has nothing in common with her future onscreen counterpart, Dr. Holly Goodhead. Gala is an interesting character in that she's a taken woman who ultimately remains faithful to her fiancé at the end of the book. However, she forms an intimate bond with 007 over the course of their mission for the sake of survival. At one point, she tells Bond that they're "in it together," and until the mission concludes, she's his emotional support even if they never consummate their brief relationship.

Just as it isn't heavy on romance, *Moonraker* isn't particularly heavy on action, either. Fleming, perhaps knowing this, began the story with Bond at the firing range, though the brief bit doesn't amount to anything. The first real action scene, if it could be called that, occurs when Bond and Gala go for a swim and survive some falling debris from a seaside cliff while out for a swim. Fleming does manage a hell of a good car chase between Bond and Drax, the former in his old Bentley and the latter in a new Mercedes. There are no gimmicks courtesy of Q Branch, of course, that would come with the films, but the chase is solid just the same.

Fleming instills a proper sense of dread and urgency in the proceedings when Gala is found out as a spy. At the same time, Bond begins noticing anomalies in the stock market, indicating that someone knows of a looming disaster. Gala knows that it's the planned bombing of London, while Bond can only assume that the Moonraker is destined to be a failure and Drax has warned close friends. Drax's grandstand speech in front of the English public, where he calls the Moonraker a "missile of vengeance" is well played. Although it seems to listeners that Drax is speaking on behalf of England, he is really speaking for his homeland, Germany.

One of the only things the *Moonraker* film lifted from the book was a scene where Bond and Gala are captured by

Drax and held prisoner in an exhaust port for the rocket. As in the film, it's Drax's hope that the two will be burnt alive. As it is, Bond and Dr. Goodhead had it far easier in the film, escaping unscathed with some gadgets from Q Branch. But not Fleming's Bond. He and Gala go through quite an ordeal in escaping the exhaust vents and end up badly scalded.

I suppose one could consider the ending quasi-repetitive of the previous book in the sense that Bond and the female lead need only to survive a traumatic physical event until the villain explodes. In *Live and Let Die's* case, it was Bond and Solitaire being dragged across jagged coral in shark-infested waters before the bomb on Mr. Big's yacht detonates. In *Moonraker*, Bond and Gala manage to change the rocket's trajectory to hit Drax and his men, who are out at sea on a submarine.[64] However, they are unable to fully escape the compound and must survive the scalding heat of the launch. So, again, basically it's just a game of 'survive until the bad guy explodes' as in the previous entry.

While *Moonraker* ultimately raises the stakes over the last book with all of London at risk, it's still a bit pedestrian compared to its globetrotting brethren, and especially compared to the film to bear its name.

Ian Fleming's *Moonraker*

Fleming's efforts to manifest *Moonraker* into a film came closer than the preceding two James Bond books—no, the *Casino Royale* TV drama didn't count. First, actor John Payne attempted to option the novel for a film in 1955, but it came to naught. Next up was the Rank Organization, which struck a deal with Fleming to option *Moonraker*. Fleming then dusted off his old treatment, added elements from the book, and wrote a screenplay that proved to be rather interesting in its historical context.

---

[64] Before he realizes he can reroute the missile, Bond considers self-sacrifice in igniting the Moonraker at the launch pad to save London.

In his screenplay totaling 150 pages, Fleming showed that, unlike many other authors, he was not afraid to deviate from his source material. For starters, Fleming oddly did away with M. Fleming also inserted a new character into the fray, that being Tosh, a Cockney card sharp/undercover agent who aids Bond in trying to take down Drax. From what I can piece together from other sources, Fleming began his screenplay focusing on Drax rather than Bond, kicking off with Drax being harassed by bullies in his private school days, thus setting him down the path of villainy.

Bond's introduction was to come with him leaning over the open hood of his Bentley 4½ Litre. Fleming described his character in the script as "A dark-haired man of rather savage good looks... wearing a grey flannel suit and an expression of rapt wonder." Jon Gilbert, an expert in Fleming literature, read the script and gave some interesting observations. Modern 007 fans consider Daniel Craig's Bond emerging from the ocean in his blue swim trunks in 2006's *Casino Royale* as iconic imagery. Coincidence or not, Fleming envisioned Bond going for a swim clad in light blue swim trunks with Gala. At other points, Fleming dresses Bond in Sean Connery's signature tuxedo. Gilbert noted that, as such, Fleming may have influenced Bond's onscreen look more than people initially thought.

Gilbert also mentioned that Fleming's habits as a novelist as opposed to a screenwriter were evident in the screenplay, which was more descriptive and akin to a short novella. *Scripting 007* and also *Ian Fleming: The Complete Man* included a few quotations from the script. The most interesting sample, and also indicative of Fleming's over-description, is Drax's naming of the Moonraker:

> [The Moonraker is] almost flashy, piratical, romantic; so that in their imagination they can picture the thing sweeping up through the night sky, ruthless, all set to conquer continents and planets,

> principalities of stars, archipelagoes of Milky Ways in a perfect fever of Empire building, the Union Jack waving through the Heavens until great areas of the sky-maps have to be shaded red, roping it all in. (Breaking off and standing perfectly still) The Moonraker! [...] The power that can help to give me [....] world control, world domination.

While the Rank Organization passed on the script, finished and dated August 7, 1956, *Moonraker* was at least adapted in 1956 as a radio play with Bob Holness voicing Bond.

Gerry Anderson's *Moonraker*

While James Bond and the puppets of Gerry Anderson's *Thunderbirds* TV series might seem like odd bedfellows, producer Harry Saltzman approached Anderson about adapting *Moonraker* at some point in either the mid or late-1960s. Perhaps it was due to the fact that *Thunderbirds* was a big hit on TV the same year that *Thunderball* was a big hit in theaters.[65] Though *Moonraker* wouldn't go before cameras until a full decade later sans any credit to Anderson, as it turned out, some of his ideas were used in the 1979 *Moonraker* and in the preceding Bond film, 1977's *The Spy Who Loved Me*. Although he received no onscreen credit, Anderson was eventually compensated in an out-of-court settlement by EON when he pointed out that they had indeed used some of his ideas. Part of the stipulation was that Anderson had to destroy all copies of his script. Lucky for us, Anderson ratholed one copy away in secret.

---

[65] Anderson's relationship with Saltzman began with another aborted project; an adaptation the novel *Cold War in a Country Garden*. A bit like *Honey, I Shrunk the Kids* but without the kids, scientists shrink themselves down in an experiment and get lost in a garden. Saltzman remembered the meeting and considered Anderson the perfect man to helm *Moonraker*.

The long-lost script was discovered by Anderson's son, Jamie, after his father's death. Despite the far-out nature of his *Thunderbirds* TV series, Anderson's version of *Moonraker* was surprisingly still Earth-based. While there were no trips to outer space, Anderson did at least get 007 out of jolly old England, unlike the novel, with Bond going to Brazil and the Caribbean. Drax's description from the novel was retained, though, with long red hair and a big, red mustache. Anderson's only variation was that his Drax was wheelchair-bound, which may have tied into his war-time injuries from the book.[66] Otherwise, Anderson was not a fan of Fleming's novel, not considering it to be fantastic enough for James Bond in the post-*Thunderball* era.

At only 84 pages, much too short to be a script but too long to be a treatment, Anderson packed in a lot of ideas. In fact, his script more or less featured the plots of 1977's *The Spy Who Loved Me* rolled into one with 1979's *Moonraker*. In the tradition of the best villains, Drax's ambitions are altruistic in his own mind: Drax intends to provide security against nuclear war via the threat of global annihilation. Specifically, the Moonraker is a type of super-rocket set to orbit the moon. However, if nuclear weapons are ever detected on Earth, Moonraker will change course for Earth and then blow up the entire planet. At least that was the impression I got from one source. Overall, it seems like overkill when coupled with the other major story element: Drax wants to create a master race that is immune to radiation, which can repopulate Earth after humanity has been decimated by the Moonraker.[67] Lastly, like *Spy's* Karl Stromberg, Drax's secret base is situated on a huge supertanker out at sea.

---

[66] In the book, Drax is disfigured from the war, and uses his hair and beard to hide some of his facial scars.

[67] Not having read the actual treatment, maybe I just don't understand it, but I have to ask, why doesn't Drax just nuke everybody as Stromberg planned to do in *The Spy Who Loved Me*? Why have the ruse of the Moonraker as a nuclear deterrent to begin

If there's one flaw with Anderson's treatment, it's that it has too many ideas for just one movie. The idea of the Moonraker orbiting the moon as a potential threat to the world alone would have been enough. "So the whole idea is, it's mutually assured destruction.... but independently controlled," Jamie Anderson said. "So once it's launched, it's got its own detection systems, nobody can influence it."[68]

In addition to its world-ending plot, Anderson also planned quite a bevy of action sequences. One would've given Bond his own mini one-man submarine to command, in which he outruns dolphins with explosives attached to them. Another scene was to put Bond in a hovercraft chase. A traditional car chase through Dover was also planned, with Bond driving his Austin Martin while pursued by a black Mercedes in keeping with the book. On the note of what else was retained from the novel, Anderson has Drax and Bond playing cards, albeit on Drax's private jet in midair, as opposed to the gentleman's club of the book. Lastly, Gala Brand was also retained, unlike the 1979 film.

The main set-piece would have seen Bond being held prisoner on Drax's supertanker, the purpose of which was carrying the Moonraker rocket. When Bond escapes onto the massive deck, he's pursued by guards on motorcycles. When Bond commandeers one of the bikes, there's a fantastic chase across the deck of the massive tanker. Later, Bond and Gala would be trapped on the ship as it sinks. It should be noted that the ship is designed to sink, so that it will raise to a 90° angle, and Drax can fire the Moonraker. The rocket launches as planned and then orbits around the moon. However, in a last-minute tweak, rather than

---

with? That said, I love how Anderson's ideas were split up and utilized on *The Spy Who Loved Me* and *Moonraker*. It also explains why the two films have similar plots considering they both descended from Anderson's *Moonraker*.

[68] O'Brien, "James Bond: Details of Gerry Anderson's unmade Moonraker movie revealed," Yahoo!movies (April 2023).

irradiating the Earth, Drax switches tactics: he plans to detonate the Moonraker at an angle that will deorbit the moon from Earth. Bond manages to stop the detonation at the last minute and, unlike in the book, gets the girl, too.

Anderson was thrilled not only at the prospect of writing the next 007 epic, but also at directing it. Things boded well for the project, too, as Saltzman was over the moon for the script. "It's fantastic. This is absolutely the best!" he was reported to exclaim.[69] If Saltzman was just saying that to please Anderson, or if he liked it but Broccoli didn't, is uncertain. All that's known is that Anderson never received a commitment from Saltzman despite receiving high praise for his ideas. Another source stated that rather than not hearing back from EON, Anderson was told EON would take the script, but he would not be the director. In this rendition, Saltzman offered Anderson £20,000 for his screenplay, which Anderson turned down because he had become too attached to the script to let anyone else direct it. He had hopes that Saltzman might return to him with the offer to direct, but it didn't happen.

Just when the treatment was written is another point of contention. Some articles state that this project was developed in 1965, but 1969 seems more likely since that's when EON finally optioned *Moonraker*. In either case, in the mid-1970s, Anderson heard about the proposed supertanker in *The Spy Who Loved Me*. In *Gerry Anderson: The Authorized Biography* by Simon Archer and Stan Nicholls, Anderson explained that some friends of his

[69] Ibid.

were working on *The Spy Who Loved Me* and snuck him a copy of the script. "I thought it had similarities with our treatment so I started legal proceedings against Cubby Broccoli, who had by then taken over all Saltzman's interests in Bond," Anderson told Archer and Nicholls. Anderson accepted an out-of-court settlement not just pertaining to *The Spy Who Loved Me* but also its sequel: *Moonraker*.[70]

Upon the old script's rediscovery, Barbara Broccoli graciously placed no stipulations on the surviving treatment. Anderson's son, Jamie Anderson, said, "Barbara [Broccoli] said it's fine that it exists, we don't really want to do anything with it, [and] if you want to talk to the Fleming Estate then fine. That's kind of where it's ended." He continued, "There's definitely potential that some day it could get out there in some form, but that would be in partnership with the Fleming Estate and that's not currently on the cards. But who knows?"[71]

Cary Bates's *Moonraker*

It's commonly accepted that Cubby Broccoli swapped plans to shoot *For Your Eyes Only* for *Moonraker* upon the smash success of *Star Wars* in 1977. However, before *Star Wars* was released, Broccoli had bought an unsolicited *Moonraker* screenplay. He purchased it not necessarily to adapt in full, but to cherry-pick ideas from it, which he certainly did. However, those ideas didn't feature in the 1979 *Moonraker*, and most of them turned up in *Octopussy*.

The unsolicited screenplay came from Cary Bates, a young writer for DC Comics. Bates established a

[70] This is interesting considering that initially the sequel to *Spy Who Loved Me* was to be *For Your Eyes Only* and was switched to *Moonraker* after *Star Wars*. Perhaps Broccoli had an inkling that *Moonraker* was in the immediate future? I might go so far as to speculate that, prior to *Star Wars*, Broccoli wanted to distance *Moonraker* from *Spy* since the film versions had similar storylines.

[71] O'Brien, "James Bond: Details of Gerry Anderson's unmade Moonraker movie revealed," Yahoo!movies (April 2023).

connection with *You Only Live Twice* screenwriter Roald Dahl and got him to read his *Moonraker* script. Bates's screenplay impressed Dahl enough that he wrote Bates a letter of recommendation and managed to get the script onto Broccoli's desk, even though Broccoli abhorred and was very cautious of unsolicited material.

Among Bates's interesting ideas was to have Drax steal a nuclear submarine and then hide it in Loch Ness of all places.[72] With his nuclear submarine hidden in the loch, Drax would do the usual 'threatening the world with nuclear blackmail' thing unless he received a piece of secret technology: presumably the Moonraker.[73]

Like other aborted Bond projects of the 1970s, it had aspirations of bringing back not only SPECTRE, but also Tatiana Romanova, the Bond girl from *From Russia with Love*. She would have served the role of the sacrificial secondary Bond girl, dying from a type of acupuncture torture administered by Drax. Interestingly, since the events of *From Russia with Love*, Tatiana had gone on to become a top Russian agent, not unlike Anya Amasova in *The Spy Who Loved Me*, which had yet to be made. (Bates submitted his screenplay while Broccoli and Saltzman were developing *The Man with the Golden Gun*.)

When interviewed by Mark Edlitz for *The Lost Adventures of James Bond*, Bates had by that time forgotten the specifics of his script and only remembered a few highlights. Among them was a car chase in a special Rolls-Royce. For context, Bond was to arrive at Drax's Loch Ness castle to pose as his driver. Since Drax has a Rolls-Royce in his stable, Q, crafty as always, builds Bond a replacement Rolls-Royce to do the job in. This comes in handy when Bond splits the car in half, leaving two deadly assassins

---

[72] How or even if the Loch Ness Monster played into the story, I do not know, but the idea of underwater tunnels leading from the lake into the sea, which serves as a theory for how the Loch Ness Monster disappears so often, would have been used to smuggle the sub into the loch.

[73] What the Moonraker was in this script, Bates has forgotten.

behind in the backseat as he speeds away in the front half.[74] On the note of the assassins that Bond leaves behind, they were twins named Pluto and Plato who served as Drax's main henchmen, and who would eventually end up in *Octopussy*. The only real mystery left to solve about Bates's screenplay is how did the Moonraker of the title actually figure into the story?

DEVELOPING EON's *MOONRAKER*

After several aborted takeoffs, *Moonraker* finally made it to the big screen in 1979, in large part due to the success of *Star Wars*. Ultimately, the property was chosen for its title more than anything else, and the only major elements to carry over from the book was Drax himself and the scene where Bond and the leading lady were nearly scalded alive in the Moonraker launch chamber. Otherwise, the book and the movie have nothing in common.

When it came time to adapt *Moonraker*, Broccoli had Tom Mankiewicz kick things off. To be clear, Mankiewicz was never going to write the entire script, just get it rolling. To help them get started, Mankiewicz took a tour of NASA with Broccoli and also director Lewis Gilbert, which gave them the needed inspiration to get the script off the ground. (As such, I would guess Mankiewicz is responsible for scenes with Bond at Drax's installation early on.)

Apparently, early ideas saw Drax based out of India, as location scouting was done there to find a castle suitable for him in the Kashmir region. As usual, some but not all ideas pitched for this film trickled down into the sequels. Among those that never did was a bow and arrow toting female assassin called "The Archer," who, after assassinating a target with a poisoned butterfly brooch,[75]

[74] If this inspired the half-car chase in *A View to a Kill*, I do not know, but it's certainly possible.

[75] While the poisoned brooch would later appear in *A View to Kill* courtesy of Grace Jone's May Day, otherwise "The Archer" doesn't

is killed during a chase across the Taj Mahal. Lastly, there was also supposed to be an elaborate ski chase through the Himalayas.

Although none of these ideas were bad, it was best that India went unutilized so as to save it for *Octopussy*. And, another ski sequence would've been repetitive of *The Spy Who Loved Me*, even if it was in a different locale. Before leaving Mankiewicz behind, it's interesting to note that he stated that he never envisioned any part of the picture taking place in outer space. Odder yet, these early scripts were still entitled "For Your Eyes Only" despite featuring scenes with the Moonraker shuttle.

One of these early "For Your Eyes Only"-titled-treatments was similar to *Moonraker*, opening with the same sequence of the stolen shuttle and Bond in a freefall. However, before going to see Drax in California, as in *A View to a Kill*, Bond first has to visit a contact at the Eiffel Tower in Paris. Basically, the same scene from *A View to a Kill* plays out—obviously with altered dialogue about Drax as opposed to Zoran—and features a female assassin who Bond chases through Paris. Ultimately, she dies in Bond's arms before he can ask her any questions. When a taxicab driver pulls up next to Bond and asks if he needs a ride, Bond says, "Yes. Drop madame off at the morgue."

The next script by Christopher Wood is an absolute monster that would've ran three hours long had it been shot, which probably would've been impossible to begin with. If you want a blow-by-blow of that script, I would again suggest *Scripting 007*, but as for the most notable differences, they are as follows. Firstly, and perhaps in trying to adhere to the novel, when Bond first visits Drax's estate, Drax tells Bond that he fears a saboteur is among his employees. (By contrast, in the finished film, Drax seems annoyed that Bond is even there.) Notably, the gondola chase through Venice was much more elaborate.

---

really resemble May Day. As an aside, the idea had been considered earlier for *The Spy Who Loved Me* as well.

As if the tricked-out gondola courtesy of Q Branch wasn't enough, Moore's Bond would have pulled a *Thunderball* after the canal chase was over and taken to the skies in a jet pack. Not content to merely escape like Connery did, Moore's 007 would have been pursued by a helicopter with a machine gun mounted on it in an aerial chase. As with any Moore-era set piece, it would have a humorous conclusion. After Bond destroys the chopper, he crashes through the glass roof of a restaurant. Taking a seat, Bond says to a shocked waiter, "I'm afraid I don't have a reservation."

As if the jet pack wasn't overkill enough, the initial plan for the Rio de Janeiro sequence was to have Bond driving a DeLorean and also for Pelé to appear as one of Bond's allies. (Yes, that Pelé of soccer fame, and it's unclear if he was to be playing himself or just a footballer/secret agent in general.) Odder still, the character of Manuela is absent entirely, and in her place is a male assistant for Bond named Miguel. Notably, poor Miguel falls victim to Jaws's jaws. (In the final film, it was decided to not have Jaws kill anyone since he was going to make the switch to being a good guy in the third act.) Furthermore, Jaws is not given a love interest—nor did screenwriter Christopher Wood care for the character's insertion into the next draft.

Like the final film, Bond and Dr. Goodhead eventually find themselves captured after their tussle with Jaws in Rio de Janeiro. Instead of waking up in an ambulance, they awaken on a yacht owned by Drax. While eating an English breakfast, Drax informs Bond that he plans to drag him and Dr. Goodhead behind his yacht across the coral reef so that their blood can draw the sharks. (That's right, the famous scene from *Live and Let Die* almost ended up in *Moonraker*!) When Bond tells Drax that he's a sick man, Drax replies, "Not as sick as you are going to be, Mr. Bond."

How Bond gets out of the situation is a bit contrived. For context, Drax had earlier sent Jaws to Bond's hotel room to do some reconnaissance work. Thinking that it might have something of importance inside it, Jaws brings back a briefcase belonging to Bond. Drax commands Bond to open the briefcase, which proves to have nothing of interest inside. However, in opening the case, Bond arms a timed explosion—it's a Q Branch briefcase, after all. Although you would think that Drax would want to stay and watch Bond and Goodhead get eaten alive, lucky for Bond, Drax has business elsewhere and leaves.

Therefore, as in the *Live and Let Die* novel, Bond need only survive until the bomb detonates and destroys the yacht. This, too, is played for laughs on the part of Jaws. As Bond and Goodhead are dragged behind the yacht, Jaws would pick up the briefcase, notice that it's counting down, and put two and two together that it's an explosive. In a scene that would have strained credibility even more than Jaws falling into the circus tent without a parachute, Jaws would survive the explosion head-on. That is to say, from a distance, Bond and Goodhead watch the yacht completely explode. And yet, Jaws would be found floating amongst the debris, clutching the handle of the briefcase, thus implying that the bomb destroyed the entire yacht but not Jaws. Yes, it is funny, but it's not worth the toll it would've taken on the film. Furthermore, it would've seemed a bit repetitive to have another scene of Jaws having to escape from a shark like he did in *The Spy Who Loved Me*, as the sequence was to end with him paddling away from the shark-infested waters.

Before going any further, I want everyone to keep in mind that this script has been following the finished *Moonraker* only with added action sequences. This will make the next sequence seem even more like overkill. After surviving the exploding yacht, Bond and Goodhead have a rendezvous with Q driving a horse trailer. Inside of the trailer are two sets of the mini-jets that would appear in *Octopussy*, one for Goodhead and one for Bond. The duo take off in their respective mini-jets, leaving behind a fretting Q. Together, they trail one of Drax's transport jets.

Drax naturally sends jets of his own to intercept Bond and Goodhead. Thus, a dogfight ensues. The fight ends with Bond and Goodhead separated when the latter's jet gets shot down and crashes into a lake. Although I thought perhaps the scene would end here with Bond going down as well, the script just keeps on going. As in *Octopussy*, Bond's flight is terminated not by enemy fire, but by an empty fuel gauge. In a gag that would carry over to *Octopussy*, Bond lands the jet at a rural gas station. Following this, we would find Bond on horseback to the theme from *The Magnificent Seven,* riding to a ranch where he rendezvouses with Q, Moneypenny, and M. Amazingly, after all that, Wood includes the Amazon River boat chase, too. In this case, Bond goes to investigate the wreckage of Goodhead's plane and is intercepted by Jaws and the other boat crews as in the film.

Things proceed as in the finished film: Bond escapes via hang-glider and is lured to Drax's base by beautiful women in the jungle. Ironically, in spite of just how movie-like (i.e. overblown and illogical) the script is, it includes a clever nod to movie clichés. When Bond asks Drax what his master plan is, the villain replies: "It is a convention of the fiction beloved by parlour maids that the villain explains all before disposing of his victims. I do not intend to follow that precedent."[76] (That clever little quip aside, the script has been so preoccupied with its action sequences that it flat-out forgets to explain why Drax stole one of his own shuttles like the final film did.)

From here, things proceed as normal until we get to the space station, which is much more elaborate—and possibly R-rated. Although I'm sure it would've been filmed tastefully, aboard the space station, Bond and Goodhead were to peer into a zero-gravity chamber where two of the beautiful couples were already making love to create Drax's master race. Speaking of love, this screenplay doesn't feature Dolly, Jaws' blonde, pigtailed love interest. If you'll recall, in the final film, Bond uses Dolly to convince Jaws to switch sides. Somehow or another, Bond still

---

[76] Feutry, *Scripting 007*, p.697.

manages to win Jaws over to his cause in this script.[77] Furthermore, when Drax gets pushed into the airlock chamber, Jaws stops Bond from pulling the release lever so that he can do it himself. Although there wasn't any animosity between Drax and Jaws in the finished film, or this proto-script that I'm aware of, Jaws was to pull the lever and offer a toothy smile once Drax sails off into space.

Despite there being no short blonde love interest, Jaws still finds love before the script concludes. When he disconnects the shuttle for Bond and Goodhead, their last visual of Jaws is of him standing near a very tall, attractive redheaded woman, thus implying Jaws has found his match. Jaws' ultimate fate, however, is unknown, and from then on, there are no more differences worth discussing.

A script of that magnitude probably would have cost more to make than it would've ever grossed back—revisions were necessary. The next script is close enough to the finished film that it doesn't warrant discussion apart from a surprise cameo debatable in its merit. In the finished film, you might recall that General Gogol gets a phone call. However, the general seems more interested in the beautiful woman in his bed than he is the looming apocalypse. In this script's case, the beautiful woman is none other than General Amasova! Overall, judging by her character in *The Spy Who Loved Me*, it seems unlikely that she would hop into bed with Gogol. As for one last aside, instead of having Jaws speak in his last scene, there would've been a few humorous bits where Jaws speaks subtitled gibberish. Thankfully, that idea was omitted, too.

In retrospect, even the joke-loving Tom Mankiewicz called the finished *Moonraker* film "total camp." While I may not say that about the final film myself, I wholeheartedly agree with that sentiment whereas the two proto-scripts just discussed are concerned.

---

[77] In the film, Bond implies to Jaws that he and Dolly are not up to Drax's standards of physical perfection. Thus, fearing Drax will one day execute Dolly and himself, Jaws switches sides.

DEVELOPING 007

RELEASE DATE: June 1979
RUNTIME: 126 Minutes
DIRECTOR: Lewis Gilbert
PRODUCER: Albert R. Broccoli
SCREENPLAY: Christopher Wood
MUSIC: John Barry
CAST: Roger Moore (James Bond) Lois Chiles (Dr. Holly Goodhead) Michael Lonsdale (Hugo Drax) Richard Kiel (Jaws) Corinne Cléry (Corinne Dufour), Emily Bolton (Manuela) Toshiro Suga (Chang) Bernard Lee (M) Lois Maxwell (Moneypenny) Desmond Llewelyn (Q)

WATCHING *MOONRAKER* (1979)

1979's *Moonraker* is a lot of fun if one shuts off their brain and just goes along for the ride. But it's not Bond's fault for the lack of logic. It's Drax's. Case in point: visually the idea of a space launch base hidden inside of a Mayan temple in the jungle is superb. But it makes no sense to build a secret base in what would probably be a tourist attraction. If anything, it seems more like something the gaudy Drax of the novel would do. As it is, the boisterous Drax of the book, who Bond likened to a circus ringmaster, is a far cry from Michael Lonsdale's restrained portrayal for the film. Lonsdale, well-known for performances in other spy thrillers like *Day of the Jackal*, is positively superb as Drax, his poor choice of secret base locations aside. Second only to the famous "No, I expect you to die," line from *Goldfinger* is Drax's uttering of the line, "Look after Mr. Bond. See that some harm comes to him." Or, later, after defeating Drax's pet python: "Mr. Bond, you defy all my attempts to plan an amusing death for you."

As stated earlier, the Bond girl from the book was done away with entirely. Though Gala Brand was a sexy name in its own right, Bond girl names had become double-entendres ever since Pussy Galore. And so, Gala Brand undercover policewoman became Dr. Holly Goodhead, undercover CIA agent. While somewhat repetitive in that the female lead is another government agent for the third film in a row, Holly Goodhead holds her own like Major Amasova and unlike Miss Goodnight at least. Speaking of being repetitive, while usually it would be odd to have the same henchman twice in a row, it's nothing but a delight to see Jaws return. Apparently, kids loved him, and they also wanted to see him become a "goodie" instead of a "baddie," and in a rather endearing third act twist, he does. Call it campy if you want, but Jaws switching sides was awesome fun, especially for child audiences. Regarding the Mi6 characters, this turned out to be Bernard Lee's last outing as M, and thankfully he gets more to do than just sit around the office, accompanying Bond into the field at one point. (Actually, while they don't play bridge together, Bond and M going out to inspect Drax's lab does at least offer some semblance to the book, I suppose.)

In terms of action, *Moonraker* almost has too much of it. Unlike some Bond films, which had what you might consider an A action scene and a B action scene—think the double-decker bus chase (B.) vs. the bayou boat chase (A.) in *Live and Let Die*—*Moonraker's* action scenes are mostly A's. You've got Bond skydiving sans a parachute right off the bat, and that's a hard act to follow. The gondola scene is amusing, the boat chase through the Amazon is epic, and it's all capped off by an even grander outer space climax. Again, it's an absolute wonder that Broccoli pulled this movie off.

The finished film was the monster hit that was hoped for. If the *Spy Who Loved Me* had been Roger Moore's equivalent of *Goldfinger*, then *Moonraker* was certainly his *Thunderball*. (On that note, the end set piece is very much like *Thunderball*'s only in outer space, with astronauts replacing the frogmen.) However, Broccoli realized that he had literally taken Bond too far, and something more grounded would be necessary in the follow-up, so he would return to the film he originally planned to produce: *For Your Eyes Only*.

DIAMONDS ARE FOREVER

PUBLICATION DATE: March 26, 1956
ORIGINAL PAGE LENGTH: 257pp.
PUBLISHER: Jonathan Cape

For many, 1971's *Diamonds Are Forever* will always be "the one where Bond went to Vegas." Or, maybe, "the one where Connery came back." Those are its two most notable attributes: its location and the return of star Sean Connery after a four-year absence. It also marked the start of a sillier era for 007, despite Roger Moore often taking the blame for Bond's campier phase that lasted up until the mid-1980s. *Diamonds Are Forever*'s lighter tone isn't necessarily a bad thing, though, and, for the most part, the film's jokes all land. However, for some, *Diamonds* was a bit off-putting due to being such a departure from its more serious predecessor, the beloved *On Her Majesty's Secret Service* of 1969.

For me, the appeal of *Diamonds Are Forever* was in seeing Bond travel to the desert Southwest, Nevada being the closest 007 might ever come to my home state of New Mexico (where he admittedly would have been out of place). While distinctly Southwestern, the glit and glam of

Las Vegas still fits Bond to a tee. Upon finally reading Fleming's novel, I was quite surprised to see that Bond didn't spend as much time in Las Vegas as I assumed. And while I was aware that the book featured neither Blofeld nor diamond-encrusted, laser-shooting satellites, the novel's choice of villains took me by surprise in the form of the Spangled Mob, which was a departure from Fleming's past, more grandiose villains.

WRITING *DIAMONDS ARE FOREVER*

For Ian Fleming, *Diamonds Are Forever* started with the title itself when the author saw an advertisement reading "A diamond is forever" on a trip to New York in March 1954. Not long after for the *Sunday Times,* he reported on the fifth-largest diamond in the world. And with that, the notion that Bond's next adventure would revolve around diamonds was set.

Either because he was tired of SMERSH or because he just didn't know how to work them into the plot, Fleming settled on the American mob operating out of New York and Las Vegas as the villains. The story is a fairly simple affair, kicked into motion by a diamond smuggling operation out of Africa, necessitating that Bond pose as the diamond smuggler Peter Franks. Bond travels to New York to work with Tiffany Case, a professional diamond smuggler who works for the Spangled Mob. To compensate Bond for a job well done, the mob pays him by way of a rigged horse race. Bond and Felix Leiter then rig the race themselves so the mob-backed horse loses. The trail of diamonds eventually leads Bond to Serafino Spang, one of the two bosses of the Spangled Mob, in Las Vegas, who Bond eliminates with Tiffany Case's help. The duo boards an ocean liner, survives an assassination attempt by homosexual hitman team Wint and Kidd, and then Bond kills the other Spang brother, Jack, in Sierra Leone, Africa, thus taking down the Spangled Mob for good. Case closed.

According to Fergus Fleming, Ian Fleming's nephew, his uncle "worked harder on this novel than he had for the previous three."[78] Fleming watched the cutting and sorting of diamonds firsthand and even consulted with Sir Percy Sillitoe, the ex-head of MI5 who had run the International Diamond Security Organization. In August 1954, he made a return trip to America, specifically to Vermont, to visit old friend Ernie Cuneo, whom he named a character in the book after.[79] With Cuneo, Fleming toured the racetracks of Saratoga and some mud baths he wanted to feature in the story. While those two locations didn't make it into the film adaptation, they featured very prominently in the finished novel.[80]

Perhaps the oddest bit of trivia regarding the *Diamonds Are Forever* novel versus the film is that Fleming briefly considered including a millionaire character named Willard Whyte, who does end up in the film but not the novel. This fictional character was based upon a millionaire by the name of William Woodward Junior, whom Fleming met on his trip. The two became friendly enough that Woodward confided to Fleming that he worried that his former showgirl wife was "of the wrong social category."[81] Fleming passed along his opinion that perhaps Woodward should divorce her, and consequently, the woman shot Woodward dead. However, while the Whyte character inspired by Woodward didn't make it into the *Diamonds Are Forever* book, Woodward's car became Felix Leiter's mode of transportation. It was a special hybrid car combining the engine of a Studebaker with the luxury of a Cadillac and called a Studillac.

Fleming returned to America yet again in November, taking the train from New York to Chicago to Los Angeles

[78] Fleming, *Man with the Golden Typewriter*, p.93.

[79] Notably, though a significant character in the book called Cureo, there wasn't much room for him in the film version, so he got the ax.

[80] Yes, Blofeld takes a deadly dip in a mud bath, but it's not really similar to the scene in the novel.

[81] Fleming, *Man with the Golden Typewriter*, p.93.

and then to Las Vegas. Actually, the trip to Los Angeles coincided with a film option on *Moonraker* via Fleming's agent "Swanee" Swanson. The man who had optioned *Moonraker* for $1000 was John Payne, a relatively unknown actor. But, as stated in the previous chapter, nothing came of the negotiations, though it did allow Fleming an additional reason for visiting America and touring Las Vegas.[82] By January 1955, Fleming was back at Goldeneye typing away at *Diamonds Are Forever* while that April would see the publication of *Moonraker*.

Diamonds Are Forever beat Fleming's usual April release window and debuted courtesy of Jonathan Cape in the United Kingdom on March 26, 1956.[83] The title was another success, and Fleming knew that James Bond wouldn't be slowing down anytime soon.

READING *DIAMONDS ARE FOREVER*

After reading *Diamonds Are Forever*, and compared to *Moonraker*'s EON adaptation, I was surprised at how much of the *Diamonds* novel turned up in its 1971 film version. For instance, the book's first scene prominently features a scorpion and a helicopter in the African desert, even if the scorpion isn't dropped down anyone's shirt and the helicopter doesn't explode. Apart from the main villains, that being the Spangled Mob, nearly all of the characters carried over into the film, right down to Bond impersonating Peter Franks.[84] There are differences, of course: Mr. Wint is Mr. Winter, Kidd's first name is "Boofy," and Shady Tree is a red-headed

[82] At least one reviewer accused Fleming of padding the book via descriptions of Las Vegas, though Fleming defended this stating that he found Las Vegas so fascinating that he couldn't help it.

[83] Additionally, Fleming's research for *Diamonds Are Forever* resulted in a nonfiction book entitled *The Diamond Smugglers* (1957).

[84] The real Peter Franks never appears on-page in the book as he has been detained by the police—so no elevator-fight between Bond and Franks as in the movie.

hunchback based out of New York as opposed to a Las Vegas comedian. Felix Leiter features prominently as he does in the film, but with a hook hand since he lost part of an arm in *Live and Let Die*. No longer eligible for the CIA, Leiter now works as a P.I. for Pinkertons.

This may only be coincidental, but considering Blofeld experiences death by mud bath in the film's pre-credit sequence, it seems worth mentioning that Bond visits a mud bath establishment midway through the book. Instead of killing a bad guy, Bond witnesses bad guys Wint and Kidd sear a man with scalding hot mud. (The man was a jockey who didn't win a race to the mob's liking.) On that note, completely excised from the film version was a significant subplot where Bond investigates a rigged horse race in New York in relation to the smuggled diamonds.

Surprisingly, the Las Vegas segment of the book isn't actually that long. Bond probably spends more time in the New York region by comparison. And though Bond does have a few casino scenes, the most memorable bit of the Vegas portion takes place outside of the city at the villain's lair: a perfectly preserved Wild West ghost town called Spectreville.[85] There, Bond has a scuffle in Serafino Spang's saloon before being taken to an Old West super train pre-dating the one from Sergio Leone's *Once Upon a Time in the West* (1968). Notably, as torture, Wint and Kidd stomp Bond mercilessly with cleats in the scene.[86]

Bond eventually escapes with the aid of Tiffany Case on a railway push-car. When Spang pursues them in his locomotive, Bond reroutes the train tracks to send Spang sailing into a dead end. It's a fun scene that reminds me of something from Clive Cussler's Dirk Pitt novels, themselves partly inspired by James Bond. On the note of

---

[85] No relation to SPECTRE, by the way, as they weren't yet a twinkle in Blofeld's eye.

[86] While the Bond of the films was always placed in some kind of danger in the villain's lair, Fleming had a tradition in the books for Bond to get captured and really get the hell beaten out of him worse than his film counterpart.

This cover presents accurate depictions of both Tiffany Case and Serafino Spang.

saying so long to Spang, he really doesn't have much presence in the book compared to Drax and Mr. Big of the preceding novels. Not only is his presence unmemorable when he's on page, he doesn't rack up many pages in the story overall. As such, it's little wonder that the producers chose to replace him with Blofeld in the script.

Whether Spang's hideout in the form of a ghost town with a working locomotive is truly Bond-level grand in scale is debatable. On the one hand, it's quasi-similar to the extravagant bases of the movie villains, à la Drax building his control center in an ancient Mayan temple. But, on the other, it's hard to imagine a ghost town as being extravagant. In any case, even though the ghost town setting was axed for the *Diamonds Are Forever* film, a few drafts included it and future writers toyed with Bond visiting a ghost town in later productions, notably *A View to a Kill*.

As for other observations, I think this was the first book where Bond spouts off with something clever like Sean Connery would later do in the films. After being captured in a car chase, Bond is seated in the mob's damaged Jaguar, and he says, "Nice little car you once had. Where are we going in the remains?" Bond's love for Leiter shows through again in the books better than in the movies, and as he watches Leiter limp back to his car, Bond gets a lump in his throat. After two consecutive entries where Bond's relationships with the leading lady were somewhat perfunctory, he falls for Tiffany Case hard, and early on in the narrative at that. Critics and fans alike have often said the film shortchanged the cool, competent smuggler of the book that is Tiffany Case—and they're right. Onscreen, Jill St. John's Case only gets a few good scenes before she devolves into more of a comic relief character, which some have called a bimbo.[87] Indeed, Tiffany Case is quite lovable and Fleming's best written female character up to that point, in my opinion at least.[88] While the film's epilogue hinted at a marriage proposal between she and 007—which seemed odd—it was a nod to the book, since Bond ponders proposing to Tiffany on the cruise.

Speaking of the film's epilogue, I always assumed Wint and Kidd's last hurrah was tacked on in the tradition of *Goldfinger*. So, I was surprised when Bond and Case booked a passage on a cruise ship only to be menaced by the duo in the book. However, the cruise ship killing of Wint and Kidd is only the second to last chapter in the novel, and the last one has Bond going to the diamond mines of Africa to kill Jack Spang. Bond does so by shooting down his helicopter, interesting since the film began with an exploding helicopter in Africa, and the book ends with one.

Some might take *Diamonds Are Forever*'s storyline to task because all Bond does is take down a diamond smuggling ring, going above and beyond to do so mostly to set Tiffany free. However, it was probably never Fleming's intent to have Bond save the world every consecutive entry, as was usually the case with the films, so smuggled diamonds aren't a bad departure. It's only the Spang brothers, lacking in their presence compared to previous villains, who bring the book down a notch.

---

[87] This wasn't Jill St. John's fault. She played the character well when it was written well, notably in her first scene, but as the film progressed, her character lost steam.

[88] Bond has a rather interesting line when Tiffany asks why he's never married, and he responds that marriage doesn't "add two people together. They subtract one from the other."

James Bond: Agent of SPECTRE

While *Diamonds Are Forever* was being forged in the fires of "Development Hell" it went through a myriad of concepts that differed greatly from the final product. Included among the milieu of ideas was the "return" of Goldfinger via his twin brother and a treatment by Richard Maibaum where Bond infiltrated SPECTRE to get revenge on Blofeld. On the heels of *On Her Majesty's Secret Service*, Maibaum wanted to see 007 settle his score with his arch-nemesis, and rightly so. Maibaum's first attempt resulted in a revenge-based storyline not entirely dissimilar to 1989's *License to Kill*. It also didn't have a single scene set in Las Vegas—an integral location in the novel. Instead, Maibaum placed his story almost entirely in Asia.

Maibaum opens with Bond bedding a new woman to help ease the pain of Tracy's death. Bond's phone rings and his ex-father-in-law Draco is on the other line with information on his daughter's killers. In a pre-title teaser that Maibaum repurposed from an axed sequence meant for *OHMMS*, Bond goes to a large mail distribution center where he chases down a hooded assailant who turns out to be Irma Bunt. She's killed during the chase, and Bond finds on her person a package of diamonds. And with that, we would be off to the races with a diamond-infused title sequence.

Lucky for Bond, the stolen diamonds are linked to Blofeld. The diamond trail puts him on a plane bound for Paris. On the flight are Wint and Kidd, and in keeping with a trait of Wint's from the book, he is terrified of flying. (Notably, Maibaum envisioned Wint as resembling Jonathan Winters and Kidd as a young Terence Stamp.[89]) As in the book and the finished film, Bond poses as a diamond smuggler and allies himself with Tiffany Case. Maibaum stuck closer to Fleming's version of Tiffany Case, who had an aversion to men and sex due to a brutal rape that was part of her backstory. In the book, she comes

[89] Feutry, *Scripting 007*, p.424.

around to Bond only towards the very end. In Maibaum's treatment, Tiffany allows Bond to make love to her right off the bat, though she views it solely as a business transaction. In Tiffany's own words, she only has sex for business, never for love. Her nature appeals to Bond, though, as he sees something of himself in her.

Together, the two take off for Bangkok, where the diamonds lead them to Madame Tring, a SPECTRE operative who has no love for Blofeld. As it turns out, Blofeld's last botched operation is considered a colossal failure to SPECTRE. Bond takes advantage of this and convinces Tring that he wants to overthrow Blofeld and take over SPECTRE as its new, more competent leader. This way, Bond can take down Blofeld and SPECTRE at the same time.

Blofeld has left germ warfare behind and is entrenched in a new plan to make synthetic diamonds, which he will threaten to flood the markets with unless global diamond syndicates pay him a hefty ransom. While not as cool as a laser-shooting diamond-encrusted satellite, it was at least less fantasy-like and tonally in keeping with *OHMSS*. Because the story had been rerouted from North America to Asia, the gangster Shady Tree was replaced with an equivalent character named Saye. That said, a hunchbacked character, perhaps inspired by the Shady Tree of the novel, meets with Bond on a trip to India.

This hunchbacked informant leads Bond, sans Tiffany, to a new diamond vein in the jungles. But Bond discovers no diamond mine, only Blofeld surrounded by Malaysian thugs. Ahead of his time, as this was prior to the Kung Fu craze kicked off by 1973's *Enter the Dragon*, Maibaum envisioned Bond battling kickboxers. Also, pre-dating a scene from *Moonraker*, Bond is menaced by a python in the jungle after escaping the kickboxers. Unlike in *Moonraker*, Bond doesn't get the upper hand and is only saved when a young Maharajah shoots the big snake while he's out hunting. Thus, Bond has a new ally unique to this version of the story named Sri, who takes Bond to his palace where he naturally ogles some belly dancers. Upon being offered one, Bond was to quip that he was rusty on his Kamasutra. Perhaps inspired by the raid on the gypsy camp in *From Russia with Love*, the palace sequence concludes with an attack by armed assailants employed by SPECTRE.

Following that set piece would have been a visit to the Taj Mahal for a rendezvous with Moneypenny.[90] Shortly after, and through a series of complicated circumstances, Wint and Kidd more or less manage to frame Bond for the death of another agent. As such, M orders 006 and 008 to India to collect Bond—dead or alive. Bond would end up escaping from his fellow agents, portrayed as very competent operatives, with the help of Draco, who reenters the picture.

Another interesting scene would have Bond going to visit Tring, who he discovers is the breeder of Blofeld's special white cats. In the process, we learn two things: Blofeld has many feline pets, not just one, and they are trained to attack by Tring at her compound! Bond's fellow 00 agents trail him to her lair, where Bond saves Tring's life, earning her trust in the process. This enables Bond and Draco to attend a SPECTRE meeting with Tring in Malacca. Blofeld seems too timid to attend and instead sends a video message. Despite Blofeld's best efforts to sway his followers to stay under his leadership, half of SPECTRE agrees to side with 007, who they think is a defector from the British government.

In another interesting turn of events—and predating a plot device used in *The World is Not Enough*—Blofeld kidnaps M and holds him hostage. Perhaps for laughs, M is placed in the care of a new age hippie colony in Kuala Lumpur led by a character called "The Great Guru." Bond eventually rescues M, clearing his name in the process. There's just one problem: Blofeld's plot to flood the

---

[90] Included would've been a humorous interlude of Sri taking Moneypenny on a tour of Khajuraho temple where she blushes at the sight of all the sexual wall carvings.

market with synthetic diamonds is not illegal so M cannot authorize an attack on Blofeld's base. This doesn't stop Bond from going after him, of course. Utilizing Draco, plus 007's faction of SPECTRE, Bond raids Blofeld's diamond factory in the jungle. In the process, Draco is killed, and Blofeld escapes by elephant. Blofeld then makes his way to a PBY seaplane and flies away.

While searching Singapore for Blofeld, Bond comes across Tiffany Case by chance. She confesses that she ran away because she was beginning to develop feelings for him, which made her uncomfortable. Even Maibaum admitted that he had left Tiffany out of the story for too long. Nor does she really figure into the climax and doesn't resurface again until the epilogue. Anyhow, Maibaum concluded things with a battle at Tring's lair, where she is killed in the fight against Blofeld. Bond dispatches Blofeld, as ludicrous as this sounds, by knocking him into a den of the white attack cats bred by Tring, where he is torn to pieces by his own cats. While humorous to a degree, it strains credibility. Following this, things were to end similarly to the finished film with Bond and Tiffany menaced by Wint and Kidd on an ocean liner. And thus ended Bond's brief tenure as a double agent of SPECTRE, and also Bond's quest for vengeance against Blofeld, which would be relegated to the pre-credits scene of the final film.

Subsequent treatments would repeat the angle of a rogue Bond on the loose but drop the plot device of him posing as a SPECTRE double agent. It still followed many of the same beats, but to some degree replaced Tring with a herpetologist, Dr. Li Kung, who specializes in cobra venom and whose involvement would also enable Bond to visit the famous Bangkok snake farm. It would be there that Bond would encounter Blofeld, his neck still in a brace from *OHMSS*, and fight off the kickboxers in the snake pits. Maibaum also envisioned a scene set during a large-scale elephant festival, which he noted was not critical to moving the story along and which could also be replaced with a boat chase if it proved too difficult to film. During the final siege on Blofeld's diamond factory in Borneo, Bond is aided by the two 00 agents originally sent to arrest him, plus Draco, Tiffany Case, and Q, there specifically for the purpose of destroying Blofeld's diamonds. Blofeld again dies by cat, but at least this time it's a tiger in the jungle.

The next round of treatments are also worthy of discussion. Whether it was a returning actor like Sean Connery or George Lazenby, or a total newcomer, Maibaum strove to give Bond a good entrance in the pre-credits. To that end, Maibaum envisioned the film starting in the diamond mines of Africa. It centered on a diamond smuggling dentist, Dr. Prinz, who transports his diamonds via trained dolphins. Without getting too bogged down in context, the gist of the scene was to showcase Prinz's day-to-day diamond smuggling efforts along with his deadly female assistant, Suzie. At one point, Prinz, wearing a surgical mask, leaves for another room. When he returns, Suzie smells a rat and attacks him with the dental tools at her disposal. After the fight ends, the man rips off the mask to reveal James Bond... whoever's playing him.

After the title sequence, Bond would follow Prinz's diamond smuggling dolphins to a speedboat containing Blofeld. A chase would ensue, and Blofeld would get away as it was obviously too soon for him to get caught. Bond informs M of this in London, and, though not important to the plot, Bond's banter with Moneypenny in this scene is rather interesting. In the dialogue, Bond makes light of M in an out of character moment after Moneypenny voices her disappointment that 007 didn't bring her back a gift from Africa... as in a diamond ring. Bond then teases Moneypenny that he knows someone who would like to be more than just friends with her: M. The two share a laugh at their boss's expense, and when 007 exits, M buzzes Moneypenny to tell her he doesn't share their sense of humor.

The rest of the script features many of the same beats as Maibaum's other *Diamonds Are Forever* drafts, with Bond running afoul of Thai kickboxers and Wint and Kidd. Maibaum tips his hat to the book by having Bond getting accosted by Wint and Kidd while taking a mud bath, too. For the first time in Maibaum's treatments, Bond impersonates Peter Franks as in the book and meets Tiffany Case under that guise. Apparently written for Connery, at one point Bond was to tell his leading lady, "You're a refreshing bitch, Miss Case." Apart from this, there wasn't much else of Fleming's *Diamonds Are Forever* present in this draft.

James Bond goes West

If the last few treatments were set apart by their Far East settings, Maibaum's next round of stories were notable for relocating Bond to the Southwest. This kept better with the novel's partial setting in Las Vegas, but it also tied into a new idea literally dreamed up by Broccoli. The producer had recently dreamed about going to see his reclusive friend Howard Hughes only to find he had been replaced by an impostor. As such, Blofeld would impersonate a billionaire as part of his evil plot.

Maibaum by this point suspected that continuity between the new film and *OHMSS* may not be a priority for the producers. As compensation for the fans, he crafted a pre-credit scene where Bond seems hellbent on killing Blofeld, even if Tracy is never mentioned. Bond's killing of Blofeld in this pre-credit scene satisfied Maibaum in two ways. For one, those in the audience who wanted some form of resolution for *OHMSS* would get it, watered down though it may be. And, two, Blofeld popping up alive and well later in the story would serve as something of a surprise.

This new treatment is similar enough to the finished film that it doesn't warrant too much dissection. Of interest is that Maibaum retained Shady Tree's appearance from the book for the treatment and also had him operating out of a mud bath.[91] At this location, Wint and Kidd would try to drown Bond in mud with 007 getting out of it "somehow"—Maibaum hadn't decided how yet. Bond eventually reunites with Tiffany at the hotel of the then-unnamed millionaire character, noted only as "H.H." in the story since Howard Hughes was the main influence. Notably, the character never appears onscreen, so to speak. That said, this was just an outline, though, to use as a jumping-off point. Along those same lines, it lacked a proper ending, with Maibaum musing that perhaps Bond throws Blofeld off the roof of the hotel.[92]

The next treatment added what would become Plenty O'Toole and a proper climax that would never be filmed, perhaps regrettably. Plenty is Darlene O'Toole, a stripper/showgirl who aids Bond in getting the attention of Shady Tree. Like Serafino Spang in the book, Shady Tree resides in a ghost town, albeit a real one, outside of Las Vegas called Rhyolite. Other than serving as a unique visual backdrop, Rhyolite doesn't host any notable set pieces other than Bond escaping Shady Tree's thugs, though.

While the finished film would utilize plastic surgery to create the Blofeld clones, this treatment had them as lifelike robots. To escape Blofeld's penthouse, Bond uses suction cups to scale the skyscraper in a bit that would have pre-dated the modern *Mission Impossible* movies. As for other intriguing differences, Maibaum quasi-retains the fugitive Bond aspect when Felix Leiter orders Bond out of the country and 007 knocks his old pal unconscious.[93]

---

[91] Maibaum's pre-credit scene in this draft didn't have Bond killing Blofeld in a mud bath, by the way.

[92] As for other odd asides, Maibaum envisioned Frank Gorshin, best known as the Riddler on TV's *Batman*, playing himself. Not a mere cameo, Gorshin would work as a voice impersonator on Blofeld's payroll to impersonate the missing millionaire and would eventually end up dead.

[93] The implication being that the billionaire, here called Tycoon, has considerable sway with the government.

As to a grand finale, Maibaum mused a boat chase across Lake Meade—more on that later.

In Maibaum's 137-page screenplay version, he opens with Bond infiltrating a plastic surgery compound in Morocco. Bond knows Blofeld is there to alter his appearance, but when four different cars take off, all containing bandaged men, he doesn't know which to follow. So, instead, he stays behind to pump the receptionist for information. Based on a tip from her, Bond goes to a spa to take a dip in a mud bath. There, he's attacked by a man whose face is smeared with mud. Bond kills him, and when he wipes the mud from the man's face, it turns out to be Blofeld.

The screenplay continues to bear semblance to the final film, including Bond's trip to Amsterdam as Peter Franks and so on. As always, Maibaum did his best to throw in bits from the novel. Specifically, Q gives Bond special golf balls to smuggle the diamonds in. Q also makes a joke about a wooden leg that was uttered by Tiffany Case in the book. Speaking of Tiffany, her backstory, eventually omitted from the final film, plays into this version, with her telling Bond he's the first man she's had feelings for since her terrible sexual assault.

The bit where Leiter tries to detain Bond due to the influence of the millionaire, now named Gordon Grant, carries over with a twist. Leiter more or less lets Bond knock him out so 007 can do his duty and breach Grant's suite. Again, he uses suction cups to scale the exterior walls of the hotel. Bond drops in to find Blofeld, but the moment he pulls his gun on him, a bulletproof glass wall blocks Bond from shooting Blofeld. When Bond tells Blofeld he still owes him a life, meaning Tracy's, his old nemesis counters that he's letting him keep his own life... for now.

Instead of being knocked unconscious and left in a pipeline, Wint and Kidd put Bond in wet cement, which he awakens in the following day fully hardened. Bond doesn't get out of the jam himself—construction workers jackhammer him out—but he does get a good line out of it at least. When the construction workers ask who did this to him, Bond replies, "A couple of good mixers."[94] Q's arrival in Las Vegas is also fairly amusing, with him dressed in cowboy attire, boots and hat included. With Q's help, Bond finds Grant's ranch, complete with a restored Old West ghost town in keeping with the book. Bond sneaks onto the ranch with some help from Tiffany. There, instead of the sexy Bambi and Thumper, he initially finds another stern female SPECTRE agent in the mold of Irma Bunt, but dressed like Dale Rogers. Bond has various adventures in the ghost town, riding a horse called Bronco and also fighting off a man with a branding iron.

Bond chases the Irma Bunt-type character, codenamed the Baroness, to a functioning train called Cannonball—another nod to the novel. On the train, Bond meets the precursors to Bambi and Thumper, who go unnamed and are dressed in the same Dale Evans-like Western attire. Bond has quite a fight with them while the Baroness looks on. The two female fighters keep Bond occupied while they chug along to a ranch house where Grant is being held. The Baroness, who has just received orders to terminate Grant, gets off the train while Bond is still busy with his two beautiful opponents. Instead, it's Tiffany Case who comes to the rescue, taking out the Baroness with a shotgun and saving Grant.

For the most part, things play out like in the finished film, with Grant helping Bond find Blofeld, now in control of the laser-shooting, diamond-encrusted satellite. Bond deducts that since a great deal of power is needed to control the satellite, that Blofeld is hijacking Hoover Dam to do so. (That's where Bond got buried in concrete, so the location doesn't come totally out of left field in context to the story.) Bond is right, though more specifically, Blofeld is siphoning power from Hoover Dam and diverting it to an old mine, further amplifying this script's Western motif.

---

[94] Feutry, *Scripting 007*, p.462.

Grant, piloting a military plane with Tiffany, strikes first, shooting a missile at the mine. Blofeld escapes while Bond and Leiter arrive in an Old West mode of transportation: a horse and buggy. Bond quickly interrogates a SPECTRE lackey to learn Blofeld's plans to escape via Lake Mead.

Maibaum was under the impression that Lake Mead was full of exotic vessels owned by rich gambling men, including Chinese junks and Roman galleys. Bond was to rally the rich yacht owners in pursuit of Blofeld's boat with the following cry: "Las Vegas expects every man to do his duty!" The boat chase that follows is a bit bonkers (and it apparently racked up some unnecessary costs on the finished film). The yachts would chase Blofeld until he runs into Hoover Dam and his boat explodes. But, instead of Blofeld's corpse bobbing to the surface, it's his accomplice, Bert Saxby.[95] As a plane soars overhead, Bond deducts that it must be Blofeld. Bond then water skis with some kind of an enormous kite to become airborne so that Grant can swoop down and pick him up in midair. Tiffany opens a door, and Bond crawls inside the plane so that they can pursue Blofeld.

Bond, Grant, and Tiffany chase Blofeld through the air until the latter parachutes out of his plane. Bond does the same and eventually trails Blofeld on land to a huge cavern in the mountains. As the two had been shooting at one another in midair during their parachute dive, they are now all out of ammo and are relegated to hand-to-hand combat. Bond eventually knocks Blofeld into a seemingly bottomless chasm and then utters a deleted zinger from an old *OHMSS* script: "May he rest in pieces."[96]

The one constant in the endless development process was the epilogue on the cruise ship with Wint and Kidd.

---

[95] Willard Whyte's traitorous employee played by Bruce Cabot in the finished film.

[96] Feutry, *Scripting 007*, p.465. There's a lot more to their midair gun fight and if you're curious, I suggest checking out the page just referenced.

It's here, too, with the duo tying Tiffany up in a bathtub where they either cut her wrists or are just planning to; it's not clear. Bond rescues her, and in the scuffle, Wint and Kidd accidentally kill each other. Bond and Tiffany's closing dialogue is worth repeating. When Tiffany tells Bond to hold her forever, he tells her that nothing is forever except for what just happened to Wint and Kidd. Then he looks up at the stars and at the diamond-encrusted satellite, quipping, "And except that useless hunk of jewelry up there." (This too, was another allusion to the end of the novel, where Bond muses, "Death is forever. But so are diamonds.")

As to why Maibaum's Lake Mead finale was scrapped, that was because he and the producers eventually learned that there were no exotic yachts on Lake Mead. However, per future writer Tom Mankiewicz, Harry Saltzman forgot that the scene had been axed from the script! Mankiewicz remembered:

> ...we got a call telling us that our boats were ready for the boat chase, on Lake Mead... Harry had gotten two dozen boats and they were sitting there: the boat chase had been in an earlier version of the script.[97]

DEVELOPING EON's *DIAMONDS ARE FOREVER*

When developing *Diamonds Are Forever* on the heels of *OHMSS,* the first element to contend with was who would play Bond, since George Lazenby distanced himself from the role before his debut even hit theaters. Several future Bonds were considered for the part, including Roger Moore and Timothy Dalton.[98] Oliver Reed was the name of another English actor that came up. Per some sources, Saltzman and Broccoli sent at

---

[97] *Scripting 007*, p.465/*Bondage* (#8, 1980).

[98] Moore was busy with *The Persuaders* while Dalton was considered too young to properly play Bond.

least one draft of the script to Lazenby, just in case he had a change of heart, but he promptly turned it down. Quite a few Americans were considered for the part. Adam West visited with Broccoli about Bond at one point; Clint Eastwood was supposedly considered; MGM wanted Burt Reynolds; and EON ended up signing actor John Gavin for the part, best known for his role as the boyfriend in *Psycho*. But United Artist's president David Picker wouldn't have it. He decided he would get Connery back no matter the price, and he did.

Furthermore, United Artists didn't feel Maibaum's script was up to snuff and hired a second writer, Tom Mankiewicz. The young writer was also brought in because the producers wanted the film to better appeal to American audiences, and Mankiewicz was American. Helping Mankiewicz write the script would be Guy Hamilton. Mankiewicz's first draft, dated February 24, 1971, is remarkably similar to the finished film with only minor differences (outside of a more elaborate climax). For instance, Wint and Kidd still kill the diamond-smuggling dentist with a scorpion in the desert. But, in this draft, they drop it into his mouth rather than down the back of his shirt.[99] (The duo coerces him to show them where the wisdom teeth are in his mouth to do so.)

As there were no office scenes, Hamilton and Mankiewicz found writing Moneypenny into the story to be a challenge, and so they eventually created the scene where she sees Bond off on the hovercraft. I say eventually because she isn't in Mankiewicz's first draft and a regular immigration officer hands Bond his papers. I don't know if this is because the writers were so caught up in the story that they forgot about her, but I have read that actress Lois Maxwell was currently asking for a raise. As it was, she was a bit perturbed at being under contract, not because she disliked the character, but because the Bond films occasionally got in the way of her taking other roles.

[99] The scene was shot but was deemed a bit too much for the time.

Furthermore, Maxwell had her own ideas for Moneypenny in this film that are worth passing along, even if the producers rejected them. Either fearing she was getting too old for the part, or perhaps wanting to be free of it, she suggested that Moneypenny die.

Her idea, specifically, was that Moneypenny would arrive to aid Bond in Vegas. We would see a Cherokee airplane land on the airstrip, and a mysterious woman would emerge (though we, the prospective audience, wouldn't know who it was). That evening, to his shock, Bond would see Moneypenny across from him at the roulette table. Moneypenny would peel off one of her freckles, really a microdot with vital information on it, and hand it to Bond. The next day, her plane would take off and explode. Broccoli refused the idea, and Maxwell told him, "I'd much rather be blown up in an explosion than be superannuated."[100]

Rather than kill Moneypenny, they made her the customs agent. Though brief, it at least got Moneypenny out of the office and into the field for a change. As for other deleted scenes from the early Vegas portion, one would have had Bond escaping the Slumber Mortuary by commandeering a hearse. Bond would hilariously drive it back to the Tropicana Hotel and Casino and tell the doorman, "Have whatever's inside sent up to my room."[101]

Moving on to Tiffany Case, the damaged complex character of the novel was watered down for the final script. Only in her early scenes is she portrayed as a cool, competent diamond smuggler and eventually devolves into a ditzy beauty played for laughs. In Mankiewicz's first pass, Tiffany wears a red wig at one point, but later is seen in her apartment with platinum blonde hair, which she identifies as her natural color. Mankiewicz also tries to keep in some bits from the novel as she and Bond discuss

---

[100] Pfeifer & Lisa, *Incredible World of 007* p.207.

[101] In the interest of being thorough, this actually appeared in a later rewrite and wasn't a part of this particular draft.

how to smuggle the diamonds into America. Tiffany chides Bond by saying he better not try something stupid, like stuffing them into golf balls.

Later in the script, after Bond has arrived in Vegas, he makes a call to Felix Leiter telling him he wants the real diamonds ASAP. Leiter tells him he's with the diamonds now, as Q brought them through. Cue Q, surrounded by customs agents, who reveal that Q smuggled, or tried to smuggle, the diamonds through airport security via golf balls. It's a funny little scene, but Q would probably be the last character to get caught smuggling anything. But then again, that's partly why it's funny. Apparently this scene was revised in a future version of the script where Q smuggles them inside a fake wooden leg, another allusion to dialogue from the novel. "Ask him to do his Long John Silver imitation for you someday. It's a riot," Leiter was to quip.

Soon after is another deleted scene when Bond first enters Willard Whyte's Casino. Sammy Davis Jr. shot a cameo where he and Bert Saxby watch Bond walk in. In the script, Davis's part is simply listed as "CELEBRITY" meaning the producers would fill the part in with whoever they managed to get, be it Frank Sinatra or another Vegas-based celebrity. Notoriously, the scene was cut for reasons unknown.[102]

Anyone who reads the script may also notice that when Bond meets Plenty O'Toole that his famous line, "Named after your father, perhaps?" isn't there because Connery famously ad-libbed it. Following this is a deleted scene where Kidd and Wint kill Shady Tree, which was filmed and can be seen on the DVD/Blu-Ray. As scripted, however, Wint sprays him in the face with acid. But, as shot, he simply shoots him in the back of the head.

---

[102] Davis's cameo can be seen on home video releases, and apart from slowing down the momentum a tad, there's nothing wrong with it, and why anyone would cut a celebrity cameo is beyond me.

The most notable deleted scenes from *Diamonds Are Forever* concern just how Plenty ended up dead in Tiffany's pool. This is explained in a scene set just after she's been thrown from Bond's hotel window into a swimming pool below. After emerging from the pool, Plenty marches back up to Bond's room. By now, Bond has already bedded Tiffany (though Tiffany thinks Bond is Peter Franks). A jealous Plenty digs through Tiffany's purse, securing her address, presumably for some kind of revenge. Later, Plenty makes it to Tiffany's house but goes at the wrong time. Wint and Kidd are there to kill Tiffany and mistake Plenty for her. The duo drowns the innocent girl by encasing her feet in cement and sinking her to the bottom of Tiffany's pool.

When Leiter goes to see Bond and Tiffany, the argument about whether Bond should or shouldn't go see Willard Whyte is a bit longer. When Bond uses a repelling gun to get to the top of the penthouse, he has a momentary mishap that causes him to fall for a moment and swing over the city. He has a notable deleted line where he says, "So help me, Q, if I fall I'll kill you." Viewers will remember that in Bond's meeting with the two Blofelds at the top of the penthouse, he kills one of them. In the film, Bond is eyeing an ornamental spear, which Blofeld #1 warns him against using. Instead, Bond shoots Blofeld #2 in the head with his repelling gun. However, in this draft, Bond does use the spear which he throws through Blofeld #2's neck.

Bond is eventually gassed into unconsciousness and taken away by Wint and Kidd. The same sequence of events transpires; only Wint and Kidd have a great deal more dialogue. As the duo drives off, they decide to do "something really special" to kill Bond this time around, which is a nice touch for the characters. Many people in the real world often joke about the far-out methods used to kill characters in the Bond films, and Mankiewicz really hits home that Wint and Kidd look at killing as an art form.

Later, Bond's imitation of Bert Saxby on the phone (via the special voice-altering device) to Blofeld is played for laughs more so than in the finished film. The dialogue is basically the same, only whenever "Saxby" mentions how tough Bond is, the other characters roll their eyes or show some form of disdain at 007's arrogance. There's an additional joke in the scene with Tiffany and Blofeld in drag where Tiffany begins to cry. "Really now. There's nothing to cry about," he says. "It's not you," she replies, "It's the cat."

Willard Whyte's hilltop villa is still a ranch house in this version, complete with a cowboy guarding the front gate. Bond palavers with the front guard, who is proficient with a lasso, and we cut away to Leiter who says, "And I'll lay ten to one Bond isn't even through the front gate yet." Cut to the cowboy bound and gagged as Bond walks through the gate. He does still meet Bambi and Thumper inside the house, though.

From here until Bond lands on the oil rig there's not much to discuss in terms of differences. It's worth noting that Maibaum was disappointed that Mankiewicz had replaced his boat chase with what he considered to be a rather boring fight atop an oil rig. However, we shouldn't be too harsh on Mankiewicz's finale as it suffered setbacks that necessitated some deletions. The original idea had frogmen diving out of helicopters to plant explosives at the rig's base. (Nobody told the poster artist that this concept had been cut, or, maybe the artist drew it before it was removed since the frogmen appear on the poster.)

The biggest disappointment is probably Bond's confrontation with Blofeld, hijacking the crane that's to set the villain's batho-sub in the water. Blofeld was supposed to escape into the water, and Bond would pursue him via a weather balloon. The chase would take them to the shores of Baha, where a much more physical confrontation would take place. Bond would chase Blofeld through a salt mine and knock him into a granulator. (This would have been quite effective in light of the events of *OHMSS*. Plus, in the finished film, we don't even know if Blofeld lives or dies.

To elaborate, Blofeld's batho-sub is not lowered into the water by crane. It has a dry dock within the derrick that is filled with water so that he can depart from the bottom of the derrick itself. At the same time, the scientist who created the satellite, Dr. Metz, escapes via speedboat. Leiter and Willard Whyte take note in one of the choppers and chase after the boat. Whyte says that they need to capture Metz alive. However, one of the choppers begins shooting at Metz and blows up the boat.

Back on the derrick, before Blofeld can take off and get going, Bond gets a hold of a weather balloon's tether and ties it to the sub just before it jets off. Bond holds onto the rope, kept above water by the weather balloon, and is thus able to hitch a ride on the sub. After Bond and Blofeld zip away, we check in on Tiffany. There's a variation of her infamous machine gun scene where she misses her targets and fires into the air. In this case, she does the same thing, firing over the heads of the men she intends to kill. She hits three atop the derrick, who then fall dead onto the men she was trying to kill on her level. Soon after, Leiter and Whyte touch down in a chopper to pick her up.

Meanwhile, Blofeld's sub has beached itself near some great white hills of salt, landing at a salt mine on the California coast. Blofeld gets out and looks over the mining operation. Then he turns and sees the rope tied to his sub. He looks up at Bond, midway up the rope tied to the balloon. "Mary Poppins, I presume," Blofeld says with disdain, and then fires at Bond with a gun. Bond dives into the water and Blofeld runs off towards the salt hills. Bond chases him, but Blofeld ambushes him. When Bond dodges another gunshot, he tumbles to the bottom of a salt pit. In a reverse of what Bond would do to Blofeld in the actual film, here Blofeld torments Bond with heavy machinery, operating a steam shovel. As Blofeld tries to crush Bond in its jaws from above the pit, Bond hops onto the top of the shovel and hitches a ride back up when Blofeld raises it into the air. Bond hops down to attack Blofeld, but the villain bolts. Bond enters the steam shovel and uses it to pluck Blofeld off the ground by his head. Bond then drops Blofeld into a massive salt granulator.

Felix, Whyte, and Tiffany arrive on the scene via chopper, and you have to love Bond's one-liner, which comes after Whyte asks him, "Where's that bastard Blofeld?"

Bond smiles. "Bastard? Blofeld?" Bond looks over at the villain's remains within a salt mound. "He's the salt of the earth."

The film's ocean liner epilogue still concludes with Wint and Kidd trying to kill Bond, but by different means. As Felix and Whyte see Bond and Tiffany off, there is some additional dialogue. Bond tells Whyte, "If you're ever in London—"

Whyte cuts him off and says, "After what I've seen of the world in the last couple of days? As soon as I get the kitty litter out of my john it's back to the old..."

Later, Kidd and Wint still bring food, but try to get rid of Bond by telling him, "Monsieur is wanted in the radio room. A telephone call from Mr. Willard Whyte."

Bond goes to take the call and offers Kidd some money to keep the food warm. "But Monsieur does not have to pay us for what we are about to do," Kidd says. (Remember, Bond never once saw Wint or Kidd's faces). Tiffany takes a bite of the skewered meat, but it's too hot and she takes it out of her mouth and tosses it out the port window.

"Boy, that's hot!" she exclaims.

"Things are only just starting to warm up for you, Miss Case," Wint says ominously.

When Bond makes it to the radio room, he discovers there is no call. The operator chides him and says, "I could live five times over before Willard Whyte called this tub." An ugly realization befalls Bond, who rushes back to his room. Tiffany is now tied down to the bed and gagged. Hanging over her is a sizzling vat of boiling oil, held above her by a rope. The rope is attached to the door handle, the idea being that when the door opens, the vat will pour down onto Tiffany. They test the mechanism, opening the door a few inches so that a small bit of acid drips onto the pillow next to Tiffany, burning a hole in it.

Mr. Kidd sheds a few tears and Wint asks him what's the matter. Kidd responds, "I just can't stand these unhappy endings."

Bond is smart enough not to enter through the door, as he knows he's walking into an ambush. As Bond repels down the side of the ship to enter via the porthole, a maid is going door to door...

The suspense mounts as the maid approaches Bond's room. He bursts through the porthole just in time and sees what is about to happen. He rushes to the door and slams it back shut. Kidd then yanks on the rope to overturn the vat, but Bond has grabbed a soup tureen and catches the acid in it. As Wint approaches him, Bond tosses the acid into Wint's face and kicks him into a massive ice sculpture with a pointed end, impaling him.

Kidd's death is similar to the film, with Bond tossing brandy onto Kidd as he holds the flaming meat skewers. The enflamed Kidd is then tossed overboard. As in the film, Tiffany and Bond then look up at the stars and ponder how they're going to get the diamonds back down to earth.

Though the acid was an exciting little idea, it was perhaps a little too over-the-top and contrived—like something one would see on the Adam West *Batman* TV series. The less extravagant ending works better.

It's unknown when the original climax at the salt mine was cut, but the salt granulator scene was going to be shot, and a location was scouted. However, the property owner wouldn't give permission to film on his land. Thus, like Maibaum's boat chase, another good idea was dropped. [103]

[103] The salt granulator was initially repurposed for *Live and Let Die* as a giant sugar granulator until the producers stumbled upon the crocodile farm. It was then done away with for the final time. An idea from *Diamonds* that did make it into *Live and Let Die* was Bond using a hang glider, since in *Diamond's* pre-credit scene, Bond was originally supposed to arrive at one location via hang glider.

DEVELOPING 007

RELEASE DATE: December 1971
RUNTIME: 120 Minutes
DIRECTOR: Guy Hamilton
PRODUCERS: Albert R. Broccoli & Harry Saltzman
SCREENPLAY: Richard Maibaum & Tom Mankiewicz
MUSIC: John Barry
CAST: Sean Connery (James Bond)
Jill St. John (Tiffany Case)
Charles Gray (Blofeld)
Jimmy Dean (Willard Whyte)
Lana Wood (Plenty O'Toole)
Norman Burton (Felix Leiter)
Bruce Glover (Mr. Wint)
Putter Smith (Mr. Kidd)
Bruce Cabot (Bert Saxby)
Bernard Lee (M)
Lois Maxwell (Moneypenny)
Desmond Llewelyn (Q)

WATCHING *DIAMONDS ARE FOREVER* (1971)

For most fans, *Diamonds Are Forever* was a mixed bag. While it offered the return of Sean Connery, plus *Goldfinger* director Guy Hamilton, it did not offer a reprise of the Connery era last seen in *You Only Live Twice*. As stated earlier, *Diamonds Are Forever* is quite a switch from its predecessors tonally. While Roger Moore usually takes the blame for kicking off the campy era of Bond, the gags and jokes fly freely during Connery's return. Heck, *Diamonds Are Forever* is arguably more "campy" than *Live and Let Die*. Another reason the film is often taken to task is that it used Blofeld as the villain for the third consecutive entry. This would have been forgivable had the film followed up on *OHMSS*. Presumably, due to George Lazenby's exit, it was decided only to allude to *OHMSS* in the pre-credits scene. That Bond is out to avenge Tracy requires reading between the lines on the audience's part, though.

As for the altering of the novel, this was nothing new. *You Only Live Twice* was wildly different from the source material, for instance. While a good deal of the *Diamonds* novel ended up in the film, by the time of *Diamonds'* development, 007 had been onscreen for a decade. The idea of the big screen Bond tangling with simple gangsters simply wouldn't fly with audiences, and so Blofeld was back for a third consecutive film. However, it's not like it was any great loss to cut the Spangled Mob.

Blofeld is also portrayed by a different actor for the third time in a row.[104] While Donald Pleasance played him in a rather creepy manner for *You Only Live Twice*, Telly Savalas brought power and charisma to his Blofeld in *OHMSS*. As to where this leaves Charles Gray, his Blofeld is refined, some might even say prissy at times. His is definitely the least threatening of the bunch, captivating though his screen presence might be. As stated earlier, Blofeld is never taken to task for the death of Tracy. If anything, after Bond "kills" Blofeld in the opener, when they reunite later, they seem almost more like frenemies than sworn enemies considering their comfortable banter.

If the film had stuck closer to the novel, there was an interesting opportunity for Bond to rebound from Tracy with Jill St. John's Tiffany Case, who, in the book, Bond falls in love with and considers marrying. Of course, on the other hand, it might have been too repetitive to have Bond falling too hard for his leading ladies in consecutive entries. The film's epilogue features a jokey allusion to a marriage proposal, which seems out of place considering that Bond doesn't seem particularly partial to the cinematic version of Tiffany Case.

As for secondary Bond girl Plenty O'Toole, her screen time is brief despite having one of the more recognizable names of the series. Her cruel death also seems tonally out

---

[104] Perhaps it's more proper to say for the fourth time in a row, but in *From Russia with Love* and *Thunderball* his face is never shown, and the actor isn't even credited.

of place, not to mention that a deleted scene made her departure confusing for many viewers. Bond's tussle with Bambi and Thumper is good fun for the most part, as is Jimmy Dean as Willard Whyte. Likewise, Wint and Kidd, the only major villains of the book to make it into the movie, are interesting. They feel a bit disjointed in the narrative considering that Bond doesn't interact with them until the final scene, unlike other films where he battles the henchmen regularly.[105]

Unused concept poster emphasizing Connery's return.

As for action, *Diamonds Are Forever* delivers for the most part. The best bit is probably the chase from the Nevada desert into Las Vegas itself. The only novelty that the chase really offers is that the first half takes place in a Lunar Roving Vehicle, or "moonbuggy," which is admittedly cool. However, if the same chase had occurred in a regular dune buggy, it wouldn't be as interesting. In other words, it was the vehicle rather than the choreography that made it notable. Nor is the chase in the Mustang through Las Vegas particularly novel when compared to other car chases in films of the time, but it is very well executed and fun just the same. But, as with the moonbuggy, take the chase off the glittering streets of Las Vegas and replace the Mustang with a more mundane vehicle, and it's difficult to say if it would be especially entertaining.

[105] Richard Maibaum also noted this as an oddity.

Unfortunately, the big finale on the oil rig is possibly the film's weakest link. For starters, it's repetitive in the sense that it's another helicopter assault on the villain's high-top lair—an opinion that Maibaum voiced when critiquing the script. Likewise, instead of a bobsled, Blofeld tries to escape in a bathysphere/submarine hybrid, even if he doesn't get very far. Not only is the scrapped original ending where Blofeld escapes to a salt mine better written, Blofeld's ultimate fate is unclear. Did he die in the explosion? Did he get away? Was he arrested? We have no idea.

All qualms aside, Connery's return to the role proved to be a huge hit with audiences, putting to bed the fear that Bond was outdated in the 1970s. And, like other Bonds in the mold of *Moonraker*, it's a fun film if viewed in the right frame of mind.

FROM RUSSIA, WITH LOVE

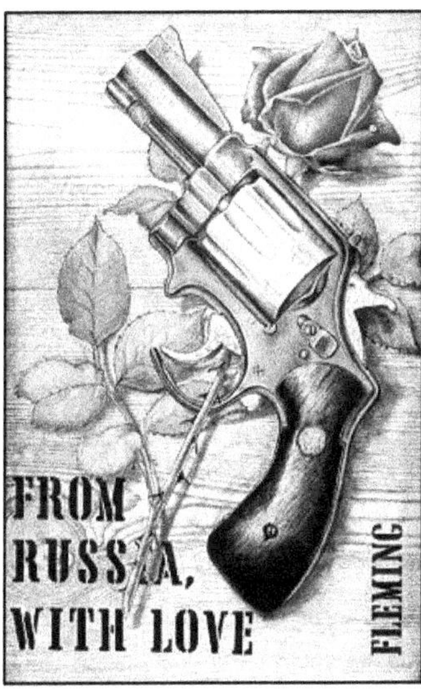

PUBLICATION DATE:
April 8, 1957
ORIGINAL PAGE LENGTH: 253pp.
PUBLISHER: Jonathan Cape
*The novel is titled *From Russia, with Love* while the film is titled *From Russia with Love* (sans the comma)

In terms of the novels, and to a lesser extent the films, *From Russia, with Love* was the 007 adventure that really put Bond on the map. In the case of the books, while Bond had been popular in Britain for some time, John F. Kennedy's listing of *From Russia, with Love* in 1962 as one of his favorite books garnered 007 a new international readership. As for the films, 1963's *From Russia with Love* was a huge step up from the lower-budgeted *Dr. No,* and its success enabled the even bigger-budgeted *Goldfinger*, the entry that cemented the James Bond film formula.

In the words of my friend and fellow Bond fan Neil Riebe, "*From Russia, with Love* is Fleming's most solid book. It's more of a serious novel than a quickie thriller like the others." I would have to say that I agree.

WRITING *FROM RUSSIA, WITH LOVE*

The impetus for *From Russia, with Love* came from a *Sunday Times* assignment that sent Fleming to Istanbul to cover an INTERPOL conference in June of 1955. While there, he experienced an insurrection involving the Muslim and Greek populations firsthand. Fleming also met a man named Nazim Kalkavan, an Oxford educated ship owner who would form the basis of Kerim Bey, arguably the heart of the novel to a degree. As for Rosa Klebb, Fleming based her on Colonel Rybkina, a real-life member of the Lenin Military-Political Academy.

The quest for the Russian *Spektor* decoder stemmed from one of Fleming's own WWII exploits, where, serving on the Naval Intelligence Division, he tried to ascertain the whereabouts of a real cipher device known as "The Enigma Machine." Bond rides the *Orient Express* because Fleming had done so himself, though his trip wasn't quite as exciting as 007's. Fleming's inspiration for Bond's adventure on the train came from another real-life incident. In 1950, a US naval attaché and intelligence agent carrying important intelligence documents was found dead on the train, thought to have been assassinated by Soviet agents. From those elements, Fleming crafted what many consider his best Bond book. Fleming agreed, writing, "Personally I think *From Russia, with Love* was, in many respects, my best book, but the great thing is that each one of the books seems to have been a favourite with one or other section of the public and none has yet been completely damned."[106]

By March of 1956, Fleming had completed a 228-page manuscript which was fairly different from the finished product. As it was, Fleming would revise this title more so than the previous four. In another first, and apparently tired of the text-only covers of his previous releases, Fleming hired artist Richard Chopping to create cover art that went on to be very well received.

---

[106] Chancellor, *James Bond,* p.97.

DEVELOPING 007

Just as Sir Arthur Conan Doyle eventually became burnt out on Sherlock Holmes and sent him tumbling off a waterfall, Fleming was tiring of Bond. Famously, *From Russia, with Love* ends with Bond falling to the floor unconscious after having been poisoned. Originally, the book ended as its predecessors had, with Bond romancing his current leading lady. In a letter to fellow author Raymond Chandler, Fleming confessed, "My muse is in a very bad way ... I am getting fed up with Bond and it has been very difficult to make him go through his tawdry tricks."[107] And so, Bond loses consciousness on the last page, his fate uncertain. Fleming was wise enough to leave his fate ambiguous so not as to write himself into a corner, but if he had wanted to, Bond could have died never to return.

Interestingly, just as the *From Russia with Love* film marked the first appearance of Q onscreen, the book's release coincided with the creation of the character by Fleming. In reference to *Diamonds Are Forever*, a gun expert and non-fiction author on the subject, Geoffrey Boothroyd, wrote to Fleming with some constructive criticism. Boothroyd was a true fan, not a nitpicker, who critiqued Bond's using a Beretta, which was a "lady's gun." Fleming appreciated Boothroyd's advice and would utilize it for future entries even if it was too late to revise *From Russia, with Love*. In appreciation, the character we today know as Q would appear as Major Boothroyd in the next novel, *Dr. No*.

---

[107] Parker, *Goldeneye*, p.208.

In retrospect regarding the late Commander Bond, to Daniel George, Fleming noted in a letter that one often got blind to one's own writings and he admitted that he was worried "the whole Bond joke might be getting a bit stale."[108] Fleming needn't have worried. It was his most praised book upon release and still is to this day. "The writing seduced effortlessly," wrote Fergus Fleming of his uncle's novel.[109] Upon receiving a deluge of mail from readers worried about Bond, Fleming decided that the poison was non-lethal after all.

READING *FROM RUSSIA, WITH LOVE*

After sitting out the last two 007 adventures, SMERSH returns with a vengeance. The first scene sees Red Grant, codenamed Granite, getting his massage in the hedge-rimmed garden as in the film. Like he does with Bond, Fleming humanizes Grant, if it could be called that. In his backstory, Fleming reveals that Grant is a deranged serial killer who was known as the "Moon Killer" in his younger days. Like a werewolf, Grant feels the irrepressible need to kill once a month during the full moon.

In contrast to the film's simplified, straight-to-the-point opening where a Bond-lookalike is strangled to death, Part I of the novel is devoted entirely to the villains, explaining why SMERSH wants Bond dead. In essence, it's a form of psychological warfare, as they feel that Bond represents the best of Mi6, and one SMERSH member even likens him to the myth of Sherlock Holmes.[110] Therefore, if SMERSH kills 007, they will kill the spirit and the "myth" of Mi6.

Even if Bond is absent from Part I entirely, getting inside the heads of Rosa Kleb, Red Grant, and Tatiana "Tania"

---

[108] Fleming, *Man with the Golden Typewriter*, p.119.

[109] Ibid, p.110.

[110] I find the reference to Holmes in this book doubly ironic since Fleming, like Sir Arthur Conan Doyle before him, would kill off his iconic hero only to bring him back.

Romanova is interesting, especially in the case of Kleb. While Grant is asexual—his only desire is violence and death—Kleb is depicted as either bisexual or lesbian; it's not clear. We get to see a more... ahem... revealing side of Kleb in the novel. In one scene where she meets with Tania, Kleb comes out of her bedroom wearing a see-through nightgown, looking like the "oldest and ugliest whore in the world" in Fleming's words.

Unusual for a Fleming book, it's a long time getting to Bond, over a hundred pages in fact depending upon the edition and the page margins. Bond's portion of the story, Part II, begins with a glimpse into his personal life, including an interaction with his Scottish housekeeper May, only mentioned in the previous books. While an amusing character, she wouldn't have been a good fit for the larger-than-life Bond of the movies. Loelia Ponsonby, Bond's secretary, has a fairly strong presence in the opening portion of Part II as well, with Bond noting his attraction to her. As we all know, the character never made the jump to the big screen. However, one could argue that Bond's flirtatious relationship with Loelia was transposed onto Miss Moneypenny in the movies.

Initially, not much explanation is offered as to why Tiffany Case left 007, only that it was her decision, and she sailed off for America. (Later, M pulls it out of Bond that she began an affair with a U.S. military man.) Bond also suffers from a case of boredom at the book's onset, musing to himself, "Those whom the gods wish to destroy, they first make bored." It's a rather profound thought for what Fleming often teased were just simple thrillers.

Fleming's flirtation with the word Spectre continues, though SPECTRE itself wouldn't debut until *Thunderball*. In the last novel, he named the villain's lair Spectreville, and in this one, the Russian cipher device is called the *Spektor*.[111] Likewise, the first true gadget of Q Branch

---

[111] Renamed the *Lektor* in the film since SPECTRE features as the antagonist.

debuts in the form of 007's attaché case, which famously carried over into the film. In the book, the case comes complete with hidden ammunition rounds, throwing knives, and a cyanide pill, which Bond promptly flushes down the toilet, not willing to entertain suicide. Otherwise, the case also conceals the silencer for his Beretta and some gold coins. (It is not capable of exploding as in the film, though.)

The novel excels in its medium, especially through the dialogue and discussions between Bond and Kerim Bey, which Fleming lifted wholesale from conversations between he and the character's real-life inspiration, Nazim Kalkavan. Some of the best bits from the movie originate in the book: Bond and Kerim's trip through the rat-infested tunnel is atmospheric and well-described, as is the fight at the gypsy camp later that same night. Notably, Grant's connection to the moon is referenced again when one of the gypsies warns Bond he is at risk of a man controlled by the moon, making this the second time the series gets supernatural, if only slightly.

On the note of Grant, who many Bond fans place in the category of henchman rather than chief villain, *From Russia, with Love* is unique in that it lacks a single grandiose villain like most of its predecessors. While the film would add the unseen menace of Blofeld, making him the head villain in a sense, the novel has only Kleb and Grant. As such, one could argue that *From Russia, with Love* is a Bond adventure dominated by what we would normally consider the henchmen. (Although, perhaps Kleb could be considered the central antagonist of the book, even if in the film she's more of a SPECTRE lackey.)

Reading Bond's interactions with Grant on the train vs. watching them is interesting in that you get to hear Bond's thoughts, notably how he disdains being called "old man" and the oddness of Grant's "cheap brogue" as Bond calls it. As for interesting deviations between the book and the movie, as an added bonus, the *Spektor* is secretly an explosive device, which the *Lektor* of the film was not. This ups the stakes for Bond when it comes to outfoxing Grant, as it's no longer just about his own survival, but that of M and his beloved coworkers who might suffer the explosion of the bomb.

Nor does Bond have an exploding attaché case to save him. Instead, it's Grant who has the gadgets in the form of a gun concealed within a copy of *War and Peace*, which Bond eventually wrestles control of and shoots Grant with. As the novel comes to a close—no helicopters or boat chases, by the way—instead of Kleb ambushing Bond in Venice, it's Bond who ambushes Kleb. Grant had earlier made the mistake of telling the captive Bond about a rendezvous he had with Kleb, and so Bond knows exactly where to go. However, Kleb is disguised as an old woman, initially giving Bond pause before a fight breaks out where she attacks him with poison-tipped knitting needles. René Mathis, returning from *Casino Royale,* pops in to save the day right as Bond pins Kleb to the wall with a chair.

As she's being hauled out, Kleb subtly taps her boots together, causing a small, poison-tipped blade to emerge from one of her boot tips. While passing Bond, she manages a swift kick to his shin. Since the sharpened point is rather short, Bond only thinks he's been kicked, not stabbed. Bond and Mathis joke about SMERSH having to get the last word as Kleb is hauled out the door, and a few moments later, Bond begins to feel the effects of the poison, unnoticed by Mathis. As Mathis tells Bond that he shall find some women to entertain them for the evening, Bond references Tania, stating he already has "the loveliest girl" as he falls to the ground unconscious. And with that, the book ends.

DEVELOPING EON's *FROM RUSSIA WITH LOVE*

Initially, and as they had done prior to *Dr. No*, Broccoli and Saltzman had ideas of producing *Thunderball.* However, since *LIFE* had listed *From Russia, with Love* as one of American President John F. Kennedy's favorite books, it was decided to adapt it instead.[112] *From Russia, with Love* wouldn't cost as much as the more ambitious *Thunderball,* anyway.

Not much is known of *From Russia with Love*'s first draft by Johanna Harwood, who had worked on *Dr. No,* other than that it would have opened with a more elaborate pre-credit scene. In it, Bond takes down some diamond/drug smugglers in Hong Kong and gets a pretty girl in the process. Other than throwing in SPECTRE and having Tania sacrifice herself to save Bond at the very end, this script reportedly followed Fleming's novel closely.

Leonard Cyril Deighton took over on the next draft, but by his own admission couldn't tell anyone what of his version survived into the final film as he never watched it. The bulk of *From Russia with Love* would be written by Richard Maibaum, who had proven himself with *Dr. No.* The biggest deviation, which came about due to United

---

[112] JFK's endorsement caused U.S. sales of 007 novels to skyrocket. Around the same time, the British Prime Minister, Anthony Eden, visited Goldeneye giving Fleming and his creation a double dose of publicity aided by world leaders. As for one last, admittedly somber aside, *From Russia with Love* was the last film Kennedy saw before he died.

Artists, was swapping SMERSH for SPECTRE so as to be less political. With SPECTRE also came Blofeld, though his face is never shown.

As we all know, in the book Bond begins his adventure moping over Tiffany Case. As the sequel to *Dr. No*, I suppose Maibaum could have had Bond missing Honey Rider, though perhaps the producers didn't want to give Bond that type of image. Instead, we were to find Bond with a new woman, though her identity would vary throughout the early scripts. In one of the first office scenes, Moneypenny remarks that she's tried contacting all of Bond's female friends and seems somewhat giddy that he wasn't with any of them. However, she eventually reaches Bond on a boat with a mystery woman.[113]

Not long after, Bond receives his briefing and the briefcase from Major Boothroyd. As in the book, cyanide pills are included in the case. However, considering they have zero bearing on the story, and because we couldn't be privy to Bond's inner monologue in a movie—which would tell us he just throws them out—the cyanide pills were later written out. Earlier in discussing the novel, you'll recall how much ballyhoo was made over Bond's Beretta in real life by Geoffry Boothroyd. Because this script closely adhered to the *From Russia, with Love* novel, this draft features Bond with his beloved Beretta again despite M having relieved him of it in the *Dr. No* film. As for one last difference regarding the office visit, the film's title doesn't get referenced via the bit where Bond scribbles "From Russia with love" across the photo of Tania, which he gives to Moneypenny in the final film.

As the script progresses, the differences continue to be minor and hardly worth mentioning. For instance, upon arriving in Istanbul, Bond requests a room swap simply because he doesn't have a shower, whereas in the finished film, he requests a new room because he believes the

[113] Apparently it was just a random woman and later the producers got Eunice Gayson to reprise Sylvia Trench from *Dr. No.*

current one to be bugged. Another thing that's missing is the bomb that detonates in Kerem Bey's office. Nor does Grant shadow Bond throughout the script as he does in the finished film. The absence of Grant is felt particularly during the gypsy raid. In the final film, and in a switch from the novel, Grant saves Bond from an attacker via sniper rifle. In this script, it's just a random SPECTRE agent. (Having Grant save Bond's life added a lot to the context of Grant and Bond's cat and mouse relationship in the finished film.)

When it comes to the famous assassination scene featuring the billboard of Marilyn Monroe from the novel, there are a few interesting differences. For starters, Kerim Bey has his assassin rifle hidden in one of his walking sticks. For another, the script specifically notes that whoever is featured on the billboard needs to be a current United Artists starlet. Of course, after Marilyn Monroe's 1962 death, the producers may have considered it to be in poor taste to feature her. Considering how fresh her death was, they could have been right, but it's still something of a shame the iconic actress's image wasn't used.

The film version of *From Russia with Love* adds several action scenes, the first of which has Bond and Tania actually stealing the *Lektor* device from the Russian consulate. In the book, by contrast, SMERSH simply gives the device to Tania. However, not only would this be too easy for the film, but it also wouldn't make sense in terms of the revised storyline. Because SPECTRE had replaced SMERSH as the antagonist, SMERSH would not give the device away as it was no longer their scheme, but SPECTRE's. (SPECTRE wants the device so that they can manipulate Cold War tensions.)

An especially odd alteration to the script is that Bond himself drugs Tania on the train. Or, perhaps I should say that Bond gives her a sedative, as opposed to both the book and the movie, where Grant is the one who drugs her. (Bond's logic is that she needs to stay calm when they are smuggling the *Lektor* across the border.) One of Grant's lines was probably cut because it gave away too much regarding the ending. When Grant observes the hidden weapons in Bond's attaché case, Grant originally was to mention how Rosa Kleb would appreciate the device, since all she has is a poisoned-tipped blade concealed in her boot. Bond also dispatches Grant in a different and more brutal manner, forcing his head down onto the jagged glass of a recently broken train window.

The climactic portion of this script is less elaborate than the film's. There is no helicopter chase for Bond; he and Tania make their way to the boat without much incident. Likewise, Kronsteen, the chess-playing mastermind who orchestrated the whole scheme, is terminated by Blofeld in a different manner. Instead of getting kicked in the shin with the poisoned-tipped boot on Blofeld's yacht, Kronsteen meets his end in a sabotaged elevator at SPECTRE headquarters.

The boat chase had slightly more elaborate (read: expensive) choreography, with Bond playing chicken with the SPECTRE agents at one point and almost running into a passenger boat near the Venice Canal. However, the simplified choreography of the finished film was probably just as satisfying. Bond's final confrontation with Kleb is basically similar but gives Tania less to do. In the film, Tania appropriately shoots Kleb, thus closing the circle of her character arc since it was Kleb who recruited her. In this first script, Bond drops the *Lektor* on Kleb's foot, causing her to recoil in pain. Bond then kicks Kleb's leg, causing her to kick herself with her own poisoned tipped blade in the process.

For obvious reasons, the book's ending where Bond suffers the effects of the poison was never considered. Instead, in this script, Bond is last seen passing out because he's falling asleep in Tania's lap as they sail through the Grand Canal. Though not a bad ending, the finished film's is better because it resolves a dangling plot thread; that being the scandalous footage of Tania and Bond making love which goes unresolved in this script.

The next screenplay added in the helicopter chase and, tentatively, Honey Rider. As most fans will remember, *From Russia with Love* offers a return for Sylvia Trench. This script speculates that perhaps Bond could be seen smooching with "Ursula," thus implying a brief return for Honey Rider. As for the helicopter sequence, it takes place at night as opposed to the day and has the chopper shining a spotlight down on Bond and Tania in their getaway vehicle. The chase would terminate due to the pilot's carelessness as he crashes into a rocky outcropping he failed to notice during the pursuit.

This script still had yet to settle on the final lines of the epilogue. While I wouldn't swap this script's dialogue for the exchange from the final film, it's pretty good. In regards to the scandalous footage of he and Tania, Bond quips, "Officially, I suppose I should present this to the National Archives."[114] Then, while floating in the gondola, Tania asks Bond what he's looking around for when he should be kissing her. "What is it you are looking for, James?" she asks, and he responds, "A camera, darling." Per the script: "He looks directly into ours. END."[115] It's clever, it's cute, and it's debatable if the producers had let James Bond break the fourth wall if that would've become a mainstay of the series from then on.[116]

[114] In the interest of being thorough, I should note that he utters the aforementioned axed line during the boat chase.

[115] Feutry, *Scripting 007*, p.95.

[116] That said, George Lazenby's "This never happened to the other fellow" line from *OHMSS* was pure gold, so maybe it wouldn't have

The next screenplay highlighted Grant's past better in keeping with the novel. However, in films, exposition is not as palatable as in books, and for that reason, it was likely cut. For that matter, several great lines from the book made their way into this script even if they didn't make their way into the finished film, probably due to time constraints. Notable examples include Kerim Bey stating that his tombstone would read, "This man died from living too much."[117]

The rest of the deviations aren't particularly noteworthy unless you're really interested in every minute detail. The only big one that stood out to me was that, rather atmospherically, the boat chase was supposed to take place on the black waters of night. Although it would've been difficult to see overall, the explosions and the flames reflecting on the water would've made for interesting visuals. Odder yet, the script strangely removes the final

---

been the worst thing to have Bond break the fourth wall every now and again.

[117] This line was spoken verbatim by Kerim Bey's real-life inspiration, Nazim Kalkavan, to Fleming.

scenes of Bond and Tania on the gondola. Instead, it seemed content to end on Bond's zinger, "She had her kicks," on the heels of Kleb's death. The camera would focus on Bond as he watches Kleb die off-screen, while music playing outside the balcony—presumably "From Russia with Love" as sung by Matt Monro—would become louder and louder until the screen fades to black. While "She had her kicks" is a great zinger to end on, the film's ending is still preferable to these variations.

The final script would reinstate the last scene on the gondola and also Sylvia Trench into the beginning. Many of the eventually deleted un-shot scenes aren't really of any consequence, such as Bond driving with Sylvia Trench, gnawing on a chicken leg as he does so. A little more interesting is Grant taunting Bond on the train with the knowledge that he filmed Bond and Tania making love. (Bond responds that they both should get Oscars.)

Actually, this final script retained Kleb dying by her own poison boot, and was changed during filming. As stated before, all the previous versions had Bond kicking Kleb's leg into her other leg, thus poisoning herself. However, such an action was easier to write than it was to actually act out. As luck would have it, Maibaum was on set that day. Watching the actors struggle to get the choreography right so that Bond could kick Kleb's leg into her other leg, Maibaum took note of the fact that Bond had knocked a gun out of Kleb's hand earlier. Therefore, Tania could simply pick the gun up and shoot Kleb. Maibaum remembered:

> I was standing with Cubby on the set watching them shooting the scene and I said to him: "For God's sake, there's a gun laying on the floor. Why doesn't the girl pick it up and shoot her?" Sometimes a writer should be on the set.[118]

[118] Feutry, *Scripting 007*, p.104/ Duncan, *The James Bond Archives*.

RELEASE DATE: October 1963 (UK)
May 1964 (US)
RUNTIME: 115 Minutes
DIRECTOR: Terence Young
PRODUCERS: Albert R. Broccoli
& Harry Saltzman
SCREENPLAY: Richard Maibaum &
Johanna Harwood (adaptation)
MUSIC: John Barry
CAST: Sean Connery (James Bond)
Daniela Bianchi (Tatiana Romanova)
Pedro Armendáriz (Kerim Bey) Lotte Lenya
(Rosa Klebb) Robert Shaw (Red Grant)
Vladek Sheybal (Kronsteen)
Walter Gotell (Morzeny)
Bernard Lee (M)
Lois Maxwell (Moneypenny)

WATCHING *FROM RUSSIA WITH LOVE* (1963)

While not a particularly exciting way to start compared to future openings, *From Russia With Love* begins with Bond being murdered. Although a ruse, it was probably shocking for audiences of the time to see 007 "die" in the first scene.[119] It's interesting how the film condenses the first 100 pages or so of Fleming's novel into only 17 minutes. Red Grant and Rosa Kleb are also retrofitted to become SPECTRE agents as opposed to SMERSH operatives.[120] And, due to utilizing SPECTRE, the *Spektor* device is thus renamed the *Lektor* out of necessity

[119] Interestingly, the ultra-realistic mask that the SPECTRE agent uses to play Bond predates the similar masks of the *Mission Impossible* franchise, which began with the 1966 TV series. Harry Saltzman was the one with the idea to kill Bond in the first scene to shock the audience.

[120] Kleb as a Russian defector as opposed to a patriot is a bit of departure for the character. Likewise, Grant's compulsory urge to kill on the full moon isn't referenced, perhaps because it was difficult to work into the script naturally, though it was an interesting touch for the novel's version of the character.

and to avoid confusion. Like he would be again in the future, Blofeld is added into the film where he was not yet in existence in the books. As to how SPECTRE's inclusion altered the story, they want to kill Bond for the death of Dr. No while at the same time heightening Cold War tensions. As an added bonus, they can get their hands on the *Lektor* device. Tania is not in on the ruse, either, as she thinks Kleb is still a part of the Russian government, making Tania's actions motivated by patriotism.

As for Bond, instead of moping over Tiffany Case, who didn't exist in the movies yet, Bond is introduced cavorting with Sylvia Trench again. (It would become unusual for the series to keep strong continuity in the future.) This is also the first entry to solidify the opening ritual of Bond getting briefed by M, flirting with Miss Moneypenny, and getting gadgets from Q.[121]

Overall, *From Russia with Love* is possibly the film adaptation to stick closest to its source material. This is especially true of the Istanbul segment, which has only minor alterations from the novel. Although greatly condensed, in spirit, the dialogue is mostly all there, right down to Kerim Bey mentioning his "friend," his nose. The girl fight in the gypsy camp was a much-ballyhooed aspect of the film, and it ups the ante as it seems to imply that Bond may have slept with both of them. The book's billboard, concealing the hidden assassin who sticks his rifle out of the mouth of the image of Marilyn Monroe, uses Anita Ekberg via the poster for *Call Me Bwana* (1963) instead.[122] While in the book, Bond reflects somberly on the cold-blooded killing he's just seen Kerim Bey commit, Connery's Bond simply quips, "She should've kept her mouth shut." It's a great line to cap off the scene.

---

[121] Although Q Branch built the briefcase in the book, Q himself did not appear as he does in the film here.

[122] Chapter 19 of the book is even titled "The Mouth of Marilyn Monroe." There could've been any number of reasons for not using Monroe in the film, but the most likely one was that her death was still fresh, having occurred only the year before in 1962.

As for other alterations, Grant and Kleb replace the two random Russians from the book that film Bond and Tania making love in the hotel. While you could say Grant bookends the book in that he only features prominently at the beginning and the end, in numerous scenes of the film, he lurks in the shadows, seen by the audience but not by Bond. Obtaining the *Spektor* is simple in the book as Tania "steals" it from her office, then boards the *Orient Express* with Bond. In the movie, Bond gets blueprints of the Russian consulate so that he can help Tania steal it himself.[123] The scene has Bond and Tania bombing the consulate, stealing the *Lektor*, and then escaping through the rat-infested tunnels with Kerim Bey.

Bond's battle with Red Grant set a precedent for train fights in the series, as it was followed by bouts with Tee-Hee in *Live and Let Die*, Jaws in *The Spy Who Loved Me*, and

[123] Notably, when he and Kerim Bey talk dates, Bond has an aversion to pulling off the job on the 13th. This comes from the novel, where Loelia is superstitious and doesn't want Bond traveling on the 13th. I simply find it interesting that, while not at all important to the story, Maibaum still included this aversion to the 13th.

Mr. Hinx in *SPECTRE*. The *From Russia with Love* movie adds quite a bit to the ending. In the book, once Bond and Tania get off the train, there's not much left to do as Bond's battle with Grant served as the big finale. The movie adds in a famous scene where, traveling to Venice, Bond is menaced by a helicopter, which he shoots from the skies. This is followed by a well-done boat chase that served as a better precursor to the Bond set pieces of the future when compared to its predecessor, *Dr. No*.

From Russia with Love has a unique place in the 007 canon in that, while not as grand as its sequels, it's widely regarded as one of the best films in the series. As stated before, it is also arguably the adaptation to stick the closest to the novel on which it was based. And, in an era where sequels typically didn't outgross their predecessors, *From Russia with Love* was an even greater success than *Dr. No* and paved the way for bigger Bond films to come.

DR. NO

PUBLICATION DATE:
March 31, 1958
ORIGINAL PAGE LENGTH:
256pp.
PUBLISHER:
Jonathan Cape

For me, like a lot of other Bond fans, I would imagine, *Dr. No* was special simply as the first 007 movie. It was not, however, the first one I saw. I was weaned on the wilder stuff: *Moonraker*, *Goldfinger*, *A View to a Kill*, etc. I'm not sure when I finally saw *Dr. No*, but it was naturally a little subpar for a child compared to its sequels. Having finally read the book on which it was based, though, I have a newfound appreciation for *Dr. No*.

I was a tad surprised to learn that *Dr. No* wasn't even one of the earlier books but the sixth novel overall, placing it in the middle of the book series. The fact that it followed *From Russia, with Love*, its film sequel, was another surprise. Furthermore, *From Russia, with Love* was a tough act to follow novel-wise, but Fleming still did it with style in *Dr. No*.

WRITING *DR. NO*

After killing Bond in *From Russia, with Love,* Fleming received an onslaught of fan mail querying as to whether or not Bond was really dead.[124] This, coupled with the praise heaped upon him for *From Russia, with Love,* led to Bond's revival. As had happened with *Moonraker,* the story for *Dr. No* didn't necessarily start out as a James Bond book, though.[125] Instead, it was the basis for a television series tentatively titled *James Gunn – Secret Agent,* about a Caribbean-based hero for producer Henry Morgenthou III in September 1956.[126] When the producer turned it down, Fleming simply reworked it into 007's next adventure.

Admittedly, the titular villain, Dr. No, was Fleming's own version of Dr. Fu Manchu, created by Sax Rohmer. As for Dr. No's lair, it was inspired by a trip Fleming took to the south Bahamian island of Great Inagua to view the flamingo colony there. Fleming found the island "hideous" and also asked, "Could there be a better villain's lair?"[127] As such, that's also the inspiration behind Bond posing as a birdwatcher. And, because Fleming and his companions toured the marshes by way of a Land Rover with extra-large tires, the idea of Dr. No's Dragon Tank was born.

It was never unusual for Fleming to engage in first-hand research for his novels. For this outing, he went to the Cayman Islands to hunt for seashells to learn more about Honey Rider's chosen profession. And because he wanted Bond to tussle with a giant squid, he wrote a history of the creature for the *Sunday Times*. Specifically, Fleming wrote

---

[124] In said fan letters for his anxious readers, Fleming drafted a standard reply stating that 007's condition was improving after suffering from a severe case of fugu poisoning and that he should fully recover soon.

[125] Just in case you're reading this book out of order and didn't read the *Moonraker* chapter, it was initially a film treatment about a rogue rocket that Fleming dreamed up prior to James Bond's creation.

[126] Other sources called it *Commander Jamaica.*

[127] Fleming, *Man with the Golden Typewriter*, p.164.

about a proven giant squid encounter from 1869 where the giant squid was estimated to weigh two tons.

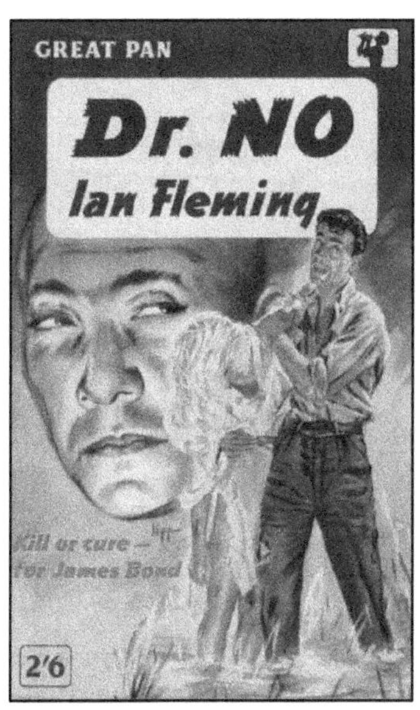

By the time Fleming was writing *Dr. No*, his Bond books had sold over one million copies worldwide.[128] His 206-page first draft was entitled "The Wound Man," after an illustration found in a 15th century surgeon's guide, before settling on *Dr. No* for the final draft. Like the others in the series, sales were healthy and got a boost in 1962 when the *Dr. No* film hit theaters.

READING *DR. NO*

At first, it seems as if *Dr. No* is back to business as usual for Fleming, with Bond appearing early on in the book, unlike its predecessor. Nor does *Dr. No* have the flair of a rich, immersive novel like *From Russia, with Love*. Instead, it's another straight thriller more akin to *Moonraker*. However, that's certainly not a bad thing, and once Bond finds himself stranded on Dr. No's island, it turns into one of the wildest rides of the series.

The book begins innocuously enough, with Bond returning to the office after recovering from the fugu poison. Due to a fan letter from Geoffry Boothroyd, M makes a bit of a fuss over Bond's Beretta in their first scene. Thus enters Major Boothroyd, the basis for Q in the films, who gives Bond a Walther PPK, which would go on to become a signature part of the 007 canon. More of a

[128] This also would've included a few of his nonfiction titles.

gunsmith than a gadget man, Fleming's Boothroyd is still easy to imagine as Desmond Llewellyn's Q, having a similar if not even sterner demeanor.

As a sequel as opposed to an origin story like the film, the book's opening hits a little different than the movie's. The book follows the trope, and I don't mean that derogatorily, of the hero taking a much-needed, easy rebound assignment—which M likens to a vacation—only to have it turn into the most grueling ordeal of their life.[129] And indeed, at first things don't appear to be too bad other than that Bond presumes Dr. No has killed Strangways.

Perhaps alluding to the fact that Bond was named after the author of an ornithology book, there's a lead in Strangways' disappearance via the Audubon Society, worried about the rare *roseate spoonbill* being endangered at Crab Key. (This is Bond's excuse for exploring the island when he meets other characters later, like Honeychile Rider.) *Dr. No* is also something of a *Live and Let Die* reunion, since Strangways was a character in that book and his sudden disappearance kicks off the action. There's even a call back to Solitaire when Bond returns to the area and wonders where his former lover is now. Bond also observes the Undertaker's Wind, which Quarrel taught him about in *Live and Let Die*. Quarrel's death in *Dr. No* is naturally more impactful in the book than in the film.

[129] The film, being an origin story, couldn't be saddled with unseen continuity, that being Bond's poisoning in *From Russia, with Love.*

There's the extra depth that a book offers, of course, but it mainly comes from the fact that, like Felix Leiter, Quarrel has a pre-existing friendship with Bond from *Live and Let Die* which deepens during *Dr. No*.

Compared to the movie, the book spends less time on Bond's investigation in Jamaica and doesn't offer as much excitement... except for one instance. While the film features a tarantula in Bond's bed, in the book, a centipede is set loose on him. As it crawls across 007's body, Fleming composes one of the most suspenseful scenes in the series. Perhaps it stems from the relatability of the situation, since most of us have had a creepy crawly scuttle across our skin before. Arguably, it is superior to the film's version of the scene.

Honeychile Rider finally makes her grand entrance in Chapter 8. Bond compares her to the statue of Venus with only one flaw: a broken nose that has healed somewhat crooked. "A dog that nobody wants to pet," Fleming at one point describes her through Bond. In that sense, the film deviated from her appearance. That said, Bond's relationship with Honey is one of the most tender of the series. He's not in love with her quite like he was Vesper Lynd or Tiffany Case, but he finds her survivor nature to be quite endearing. Bond's softer side, and therefore also Fleming's, shines through in some dialogue where Honey brings up her broken nose. While I wouldn't feel right printing the full quotation or even trying to paraphrase it, how Bond sincerely communicates to her why her broken nose doesn't matter is one of the most emotionally vulnerable and beautiful exchanges of dialogue in the series. Perhaps what makes it so good is that it simply rings true.[130]

When Bond scoffs at the notion of the "dragon," Honey scoffs back, describing to him all the wonders of nature she's observed in her years living alone in the wild.

---

[130] Later Bond will note that he's grown to love the broken nose and doesn't want to see Honey get it fixed.

Notably, she mentions a pet snake that she tied a bell to so that it could wake her up each morning. (Though not explicitly stated, Honey could be psychic along the lines of Solitaire in that she can basically speak to animals.) Like Tiffany Case, she is a rape survivor, and that's how she got the broken nose. She avenged herself by dropping a black widow on the perpetrator in his sleep and notes proudly that it took a week for him to die.

The grandiose Bond villain, not seen since *Moonraker*, makes a return with a vengeance, getting the title of the book to boot. Fleming put a lot of thought into the robotic Dr. No's description. Not only does he tower over Bond at six feet six inches tall, he also has pinchers for hands.[131] It's not just Dr. No's mechanical pinchers that make him robotic. Fleming describes him as somewhat artificial-looking and gliding across the floor in his kimono. One of Fleming's most carefully constructed villains up to that point, Dr. No's only preexisting rival is perhaps Mr. Big.

Dr. No begat the tradition of the villain capturing Bond in a brutal manner only to then wine and dine him as an honored guest when confined to his lair. (On that note, Bond telling Honey they're already in a trap and might as well eat the cheese was a line that Connery could have said rather well, though it went unutilized in the film.) Bond's dialogue with Dr. No even outshines his exchanges with Mr. Big from *Live and Let Die,* which were quite clever and thought-provoking in their own right.

While the action is fun, and the book has it in spades, for me, the most thrilling and intellectually stimulating part of the book was still the verbal sparring match between Dr. No and 007. It's the best of Fleming's dialogue so far, and the man excelled at dialogue. Dr. No's long monologue

---

[131] On the note of his hands, they are more like the film version of Tee-Hee's in that they are pinchers, which Bond thinks makes him insect-like. In the film, Dr No wears black gloves which turn out to be mechanical hands. In the book, Dr. No also wears contact lenses in an effort to trick his staff into thinking that his eyes are cameras.

doesn't overstay its welcome, and his history, mostly removed from the movie, is fascinating. As for his name, Julius No, Julius was his father's name, and No represents rejection, since his father rejected him. The rest of Dr. No's origin involves him being tortured by the Tongs, having his hands cut off, and being shot through the heart, which, in his case, is on the right side of his body. Thus, he survived.

After dinner, Bond is thrown into Dr. No's obstacle course, meant to push the human body to its limits in terms of how much pain and fear it can stand. In that regard, *Dr. No* is perhaps comparable to *The Most Dangerous Game*. (Even Fleming called this Bond adventure "old fashioned" which didn't make it "any less exciting.") Bond wills himself to survive his crawl through the tunnel of doom more to rescue Honey than to stop the rocket sabotage, that comes secondary. In one of the tunnels, Bond encounters more deadly bugs, in this case tarantulas.[132] This will come as a surprise to those who have never read the book, but after surviving Dr. No's obstacle course, Bond is dumped into a lagoon to battle a giant squid. (While the giant squid might be too fantastic for some, there was substantial evidence for their existence, which Fleming knew from writing his articles.)

Right after killing the squid, it's altogether appropriate and satisfying that Bond uses a crane to bury Dr. No in bird dung, since the island doubles as a guano mining base. The film's ending had more urgency to it, but after enduring Dr. No's gauntlet of horror in the book, the reader can take great satisfaction in 007 dispatching Dr. No at once. Honey's escape might be considered a case of *deux ex machina* for some, but I think it was well handled and paid off her character arc. As it is, Honey gets away without Bond's help—Dr. No had hopes that flesh-eating crabs would tear her to bits over the course of several days.

---

[132] The film compromised by replacing the centipede in Bond's bed with a tarantula but excluded the tarantulas in the tunnel altogether.

Fleming had earlier done a good job of showing that Honey not only knew animals but that she *likes* all animals. Her knowledge of crabs, coupled with her total lack of fear of them, more or less led to a non-event. In that sense, Honey also scores a victory on the know-it-all Dr. No through her superior knowledge of animal life.

After the death of Dr. No, Bond and Honey hijack the Dragon Tank and break out of the base. Instead of saying the film's climax is more exciting than the book's, I'll just say that both have their merits and it's debatable which is the better of the two.

DEVELOPING EON's *DR. NO*

With Bond's big screen history already briefly outlined in this book's introduction, we'll get straight to the development of *Dr. No*. Not much is known of the first treatment other than that it retains the deadly obstacle course and the giant squid, which Bond battles not only to save himself, but also Honey, who the squid would menace in place of the crabs.

The second treatment from September 1961 is quite different from the finished film. During the office briefing, M implies to 007 that the double-O program is at risk as it is currently being scrutinized by other government departments—an interesting angle to play up in the debut Bond film. Another minor difference is that Bond finds Sylvia Trench in his bed as opposed to playing golf on his apartment floor.

Where the second treatment really shows its differences, both from the source material and the finished film, is upon Bond's arrival in Jamaica. Receiving a tip that Strangways was following a lead involving rare seashells around an island called Crab Key, Bond goes to a seashell shop owned by a man named Gomez. There he meets Honey Rider early on in the shop and she is described as being of mixed ethnicity, specifically half Asian and half Caucasian. Lucky for Bond, Honey is selling one of the rare seashells which had earlier interested Strangways. The two take a cab together and though Honey is amicable enough towards 007, she sneaks off and ditches him as he pays the cab driver. Bond asks various boat captains, including Quarrel, if they know of this mysterious girl. On the note of Quarrel, as in the finished film, this entails his and Bond's first meeting. I suppose it wouldn't have been too complicated to have the duo know each other from past missions, but the screenwriters apparently felt that since this was Bond's first adventure then perhaps no previous ones should be mentioned. In any case, instead of being introduced to Quarrel by Felix Leiter, Bond simply asks Quarrel to take him to Crab Key.

The treatment retains the centipede that menaces Bond that same night. Notably, Bond also recognizes it, having seen it or a member of the same species in Gomez's shop. The script would switch back to England for once, giving M a solo scene where he receives news that moves the story along—namely that an American CIA agent was murdered in relation to Crab Key. Cut back to Bond and Quarrel on the latter's boat, where they spy naked women diving for seashells. Bond identifies one of them as Honey, and he sets off to talk to her. They have a brief exchange before being attacked by a minor character from the novel named Pus-Feller.[133] While in the book, not to mention the final film, he's an ally who owns a restaurant, in this treatment he's simply a villain out to get Bond. Pus-Feller and his men chase Bond into the dense foliage of Crab Key and to the ruins of an old fort. There Bond is rescued by Felix Leiter, who, unlike Quarrel, the writers allow Bond to know from past assignments. This is interesting because in the final film, it would be presented as he and Leiter's first meeting. But in this draft, the two reveal that they have past history through their dialogue. Leiter also explains to Bond that he's here on the trail of the murdered CIA agent.

Back on the mainland, when Bond returns to his hotel, he finds Honey Rider in bed waiting for him. Later, the two attend a dinner party that ties into Bond's investigation. The party is being thrown by a man named Buckfield, who has connections to the shady seashell shop owner, Gomez. At the party, Bond and Honey also observe Buckfield's pet Capuchin monkey named Li-Ying, which will figure into the story in an important way, odd though that may sound. When Bond and Honey leave the Buckfield residence, they are tailed by the three blind-beggar-assassins in their hearse, and a car chase ensues. As in the film, the hearse careens off a ledge to its fiery doom. Unlike the film, there is a survivor, though. Bond is surprised to find the man wearing Strangways' old watch and questions him. The dying man is only able to utter two enigmatic words: "Dragon-dogs."

Events continue to deviate wildly from the novel and the finished film. Quarrel pilots a boat containing Bond, Honey, and Leiter to Crab Key. Leiter stays with Quarrel while Bond goes ashore with Honey. There, he learns that Honey not only collects seashells but is paid to transfer messages to Puss Feller. Back at sea, Puss Feller's thugs come upon Quarrel and shoot him. Thus, he dies on his

---

[133] In the book, the name derives from the fact that he once wrestled a large octopus, thus "Octopus Feller" shortened to "Puss-Feller."

boat as opposed to the flame-thrower of Dr. No's Dragon Tank. A bullet hits the fuel tank and the boat explodes, but Leiter jumps into the ocean to safety. Before cutting away, we would see a mysterious man with pinchers for hands inspecting Quarrel's dead body.

Back on the island, Bond and Honey are on the run. They take shelter behind a waterfall for the night and the script ponders how much eroticism they can get away with. From a distance, the duo would also spy the "dragon," which the treatment notes should look as real as possible as it will not yet be revealed that it's just a machine. The next morning, Bond and Honey reunite with Leiter, who tells them about Dr. No's strange appearance. In a cutaway scene, we also learn that Dr. No, still seen only in profile, is supplying arms to Cuban revolutionaries, one of which is Gomez. The scene ends with Dr. No knocking Gomez unconscious with one of his pinchers.

Meanwhile, Bond and Honey stumble upon a cemetery at the front of which are two statues of dragon-like dogs, explaining the dying assassin's words from earlier. Bond finds two fresh graves and confirms that they belong to Strangways and his assistant. Bond and Honey are soon attacked by the "dragon," which we finally learn is just a vehicle with a flame thrower. As they are chased through the jungle, Dr. No makes his grand entrance, still in shadow, standing next to a statue of a huge Capuchin monkey. Bond and Honey surrender to Dr. No and are imprisoned inside the Dragon Tank. Inside, Bond finds Gomez in the process of dying from his blow to the head. With his last breath, Gomez warns Bond that Dr. No has loaded a Cuban boat full of explosives that is set to detonate right as it goes through the Panama Canal. This entails the treatment's main threat, whereas the final film implemented Dr. No's plan of sabotaging of the American space program.

Back at Dr. No's base, which is carved into the rock of the island, Puss Feller separates Honey from Bond, who is taken to a private meeting with Dr. No. Although some scripts have claimed that Dr. No turns out to be a monkey, this isn't remotely true. As Bond sits at a table with Dr. No, still obscured by shadow, the good doctor unscrews his pincher hands and takes them off. Around the same time, the Capuchin monkey from Buckfield's party leaps onto the table. The man in the shadows leans forward to reveal Buckfield, who tells Bond he was once a student of the mysterious Dr. No, who died and was buried in the island graveyard. Buckfield explains to Bond that he impersonates Dr. No because no white man could be the head of the Chinese gang, The Black Monkey, which Dr. No headed. (Obviously, no SPECTRE ties yet.)

Buckfield's evil plot is for the Cuban ship to explode in the Panama Canal so it will heighten Cold War tensions between the US and Russia. Buckfield's main benefit is that his Black Monkey gang can rule the Caribbean amidst the chaos. Having revealed his master plan to Bond, there's nothing left for Buckfield to do but to kill him. As he points his pistol at Bond, the pet monkey thinks it's some kind of toy and grabs at it. Bond takes advantage of the distraction to get the upper hand and uses one of the detached pinchers to threaten Buckfield.

Elsewhere, Leiter has infiltrated the base and is effectively saving the day. He hijacks the Dragon Tank, takes out several of Dr. No's men with the flame thrower, and saves Honey from Puss Feller, who he kills. Bond, meanwhile, is forcing Buckfield to lead him to the boat, which is currently being prepared for its deadly voyage. Dr. No's men smell a rat and surround Bond. Just when all hope seems lost, the Dragon Tank appears and roasts them. Leiter pops out of the Dragon Tank along with Honey, Bond explains the plot to Leiter, and they agree to send the tank careening into the explosive-filled boat.

Not long after, Bond, Honey, and Leiter all run for their lives as the obligatory island-starts-to-explode-climax ensues. The trio commandeers a boat so they can escape into the ocean. Of course, Bond can't romance Honey with Leiter there as the third wheel, and so a humorous note to end on is needed. It is presented in the form of the monkey, who stowed away on the boat. The camera would zoom in on the monkey for the final shot as it laughs and jumps.

That awful epilogue aside, even the earlier portion of the climax wasn't suited for 007. While it offered a lot of fun moments for Leiter, it didn't really give Bond enough to do. Furthermore, the idea of replacing Dr. No with an imposter seemed unnecessary. The swap came courtesy of Richard Maibaum and Wolf Mankiewicz, who both felt the villain was too Fu Manchu and too dated for 1961. Maibaum implied that for years thereafter, whenever Cubby Broccoli was irritated with him, he would bring up the fact that he "made Dr. No into a monkey." (It was from Broccoli's misremembering of the second treatment that stemmed the bizarre rumor that Dr. No had himself been a monkey, when really he only had one as a pet.)

The next treatment was a little longer and came towards the end of September 1961. It hits most of the same beats with Buckfield's party, just sans any monkeys. This treatment, too, centers on rare seashells and exploding vessels in the Panama Canal. In an early scene, Strangways' secretary, Jane, is kidnapped by Dr. No's lackeys and taken to the doctor, seen only in shadow. The scene would end with Dr. No's pinchers ripping at Jane's clothes. The seashells, *elegant venus*, make a trail for Bond again when he reaches Jamaica as in the last treatment. As for another interesting aside, in this version, Honey works for the abusive Puss Feller.

Scenes from the last treatment are present with significant deviations. For instance, Bond fights Puss Feller and his men at an old fort in the jungle until he is rescued by Leiter, who he has never met before in this treatment. Bond also sees Strangways' watch on Puss Feller's wrist during the fight as well. Odder yet, Quarrel has been removed from this treatment entirely and replaced with a new minor character named Merriman.

This treatment also adds a scene from the book that the previous treatment neglected: Dr. No sending a basket of poisoned fruit to 007's hotel room. Shortly after, Honey teams with Bond because she wants to escape from Puss Feller and her life in Jamaica. Things proceed as in the previous treatment with the boatman taking Leiter, Bond and Honey to Dr. No's island, which is no longer a guano mining base and is now a bauxite mine.

As in the previous treatment and the finished film, Bond and Honey are captured and taken before Dr. No. This one is a little closer to the final film in that Dr. No politely wines and dines the captive duo, only his aquarium is stocked with deadly sharks in this draft. In a notable scene, Dr. No informs Bond that he wants him to observe how he deals with failure. Remember Buckfield, the guy with the pet monkey in the last treatment who turned out to be Dr. No? Well, in this treatment, Dr. No is Dr. No and Buckfield is Buckfield. Buckfield is also tossed into the shark tank to be devoured in front of Bond and Honey as they eat their dinner. As it was, Buckfield wasn't able to keep Dr. No's evil plot a secret, hence his swim with the sharks. Dr. No also asks Bond if he would be interested in taking Buckfield's place. When Bond turns down his offer, Dr. No says he intends to do chemical experiments on Bond's brain. This will change his thinking process and make him more amicable to the idea of being one of his hitmen.

Unlike in the film, where Bond has to escape from a cell, and also unlike the book where Bond must survive the obstacle course, this dinner scene more or less serves as the climactic portion of this draft. Bond eventually works up the nerve to attack Dr. No with a knife, as there are no guards in the room, and Dr. No defends himself with his pinchers in a very violent and bloodied battle. Bond eventually gets the upper hand on Dr. No with the help of Honey and threatens to throw Dr. No into his shark tank if he doesn't cooperate. Coerced through violence, Dr. No leads Bond and Honey to the Dragon Tank. Bond then ties Dr. No up inside the tank, and Bond and Honey take it on a joyride through the compound, roasting the cruel Puss Feller alive before aiming the Dragon Tank at the explosive-packed boat meant for the Panama Canal. Bond and Honey jump out of the tank as it careens into the boat, with Dr. No still trapped inside, and explodes. The script would end with Bond and Honey getting a ride with Leiter back to the mainland. Notably, no cute gimmicks are listed as in the previous treatment.

There isn't a great deal of interest to be found in the next iteration of *Dr. No*, which is still fairly similar to the previous one. (The only thing that I found intriguing was that the writers repurposed Quarrel's dialogue regarding the Undertaker's Wind from *Live and Let Die* and gave it to Honey.) A fourth draft screenplay from December 1961 is much closer to the finished film, introducing the new character of Professor Dent along with his tarantula that replaces the centipede among other things. Also, the dialogue between Bond and M regarding the Beretta is a bit peppier in this script, and it would have been amusing to have seen how it played out, even if it was a bit out of character.

A lot of dialogue from the book is retained in this version, as Broccoli had complained that they had paid a hefty sum for the book but had barely used any of it. Along those lines, Honey Rider's history is closer to the book when she talks of being orphaned at a young age, her plan to become a call girl in New York, and so on. Like the peppy, humorous dialogue with M earlier, there are similar lines inserted into Bond's discussions with Dr. No. (When Dr. No catches 007 trying to steal a lighter, Bond quips that kleptomania runs in his family and that his aunt did six months in jail for it.) In the new script, Dr. No specifically mentions working for SPECTRE for the first time as well. This was done because United Artists wanted this film to be distributed worldwide and didn't want to single out Russians as the villains.

Like the preceding version, the dinner would end in a fight between Bond and Dr. No where the latter gets the better of the former with his metal hooks. After that, the script is mostly the same, with Bond waking up in his cell, escaping, and stopping Dr. No's plan. It only deviates in that Bond doesn't have to rescue Honey from drowning or attacking crabs and he simply collects her from her room before escaping the island. Nor does Leiter appear in the epilogue, and Bond mentions that Leiter is late in bringing the cavalry and to "hell with him, anyway."

After this, all the scripts to follow are similar enough to the finished film that they don't warrant discussion.

RELEASE DATE:
October 1962 (UK)
May 1963 (US)
RUNTIME: 109 Minutes
DIRECTOR: Terence Young
PRODUCERS: Albert R. Broccoli
& Harry Saltzman
SCREENPLAY: Richard Maibaum,
Johanna Harwood
& Berkely Mather
Wolf Mankowitz (uncredited)
MUSIC: Monty Norman
CAST: Sean Connery
(James Bond)
Ursula Andress (Honey Ryder)
Joseph Wiseman (Dr. No)
Jack Lord (Felix Leiter)
John Kitzmiller (Quarrel)
Anthony Dawson (Professor Dent)
Bernard Lee (M)
Lois Maxwell (Moneypenny)

WATCHING *DR. NO* (1962)

As we all know, there is no pre-credit scene and it's straight to the gun barrel and then to the credits, perhaps appropriately overlaid with the 007 theme since this is the first outing. The assassination of Strangways and his secretary soon follows and is pretty faithful to the book, three blind assassins, getaway hearse and all. This not being a sequel to *From Russia with Love*, Bond's introduction had to be wholly different, and so we find him in perfect health gambling in a fancy casino, perhaps inspired by Bond's first scene in *Casino Royale*.

No longer being a follow-up to *From Russia with Love* also changed the nature of M's briefing from the book, where M looks at Strangways' disappearance as a mere curiosity and an easy assignment for Bond after his recovery. By contrast, in the movie, instead of teasing Bond about a holiday in the sun, M treats Strangways' disappearance with grave importance and mentions that Felix Leiter is in Jamaica already. Oddly enough, the movie did retain the Beretta bit, including Major Boothroyd's briefing and even Bond trying to take the Beretta as a keepsake and M not letting him.[134]

As for more odds and ends, while Sylvia Trench was created just for the movie, the photographer girl at the airport is from the book, though Leiter shadowing Bond at the same time is an add-in. So is the car sent by Dr. No and the action scene that accompanies it where Bond battles with the treacherous driver. It's rudimentary compared to the set pieces of the sequels, but the style, coupled with Connery's performance, elevates *Dr. No* above action films of the time. Perhaps more than the action, it's Connery's quips that endear him to the audience. ("Don't let him get away," Bond says to a valet regarding the dead body in the backseat of his car.) Actually, Connery's Bond was such a novelty at the time, all the actor had to do was walk around to the 007 theme and it seemed cool.

Bond's investigation in the film is pretty different from the book aside from he and Quarrel's trip to Puss Feller's place, where they encounter the same beautiful spy who photographed Bond at the airport. Speaking of Quarrel, since this is he and Bond's first meeting as opposed to a reunion, the dynamic between the two is more suspicious and not so warm. Quarrel even pulls a knife on Bond to test him until Leiter shows up behind Bond with a gun to give him the score. In the process, the history between Bond

---

[134] Played by actor Peter Burton and called Major Boothroyd, when he was unavailable for the sequel, the character was rechristened as Q and the name stuck.

and Leiter, who isn't in the book, is rewritten entirely. While Leiter's inclusion simplified the plot for the writers, which is understandable, it's still puzzling why he couldn't be an old friend of Bond's from past missions.

Because the shooting script added a scene of Dr. No instructing Professor Dent, but didn't want Dr. No to appear just yet, Ken Adam's marvelous yet simplistic set creates a great atmosphere when coupled with Joseph Wiseman's voice over a speaker. The purpose of the visit is so that Dent can get the tarantula, which replaces the centipede.[135] Though not as frightening as the centipede, the scene of the spider crawling on Connery in bed is well directed and acted. As for another alteration, a minor secretary/double agent character from the book is upgraded into a true femme fatale who gets bedded by Bond. Her added subplot enables a car chase involving the assassins where their hearse careens off a cliff. The scene is excellently capped off with Connery's line, "I think they were on their way to a funeral." These well-received bits of dark humor were one of the major additions that Connery and director Terence Young made to the character. So was Bond's cold-blooded killing of Professor Dent, a

[135] Naturally no one would want a real centipede to crawl on them pre-CGI. Even the non-poisonous ones often have limbs that will irritate a person's skin.

benchmark moment and a type of behavior on Bond's part that wouldn't really resurface until the Daniel Craig era.

The movie takes a bit longer to get to the island and thus also Honey Rider, giving her something of a late entrance for a main character. As much of her dialogue as necessary is retained—in many cases just condensed—but the film changes her origin story entirely. In the film version, she came to Jamaica with her father, a marine biologist who died at Crab Key. She still read the entirety of the encyclopedia though, and her rape story is included too, black widow and all. All things considered, her history was condensed nicely, and her father's death at Crab Key better ties her to the story.

The Dragon Tank is nicely done for a relatively low-budget affair, and that goes double for Dr. No's control room and dining room sets. The portion of the film confined to Dr. No's lair follows the book closely, including the hospitality of the staff. And while Dr. No may not glide into Bond's room in his kimono, he does pay him a visit in his sleep like in the book. As to Dr. No's backstory, his hands weren't removed by the Tongs and in this case, his experiments are to blame for the loss of his hands. Nor is there mention of Dr. No's right-sided heart or contact lenses.[136] Overall, the spirit of Dr. No and Bond's dialogue is there, just shortened. Honey is taken away at Bond's suggestion where it is not in the book. (The "stupid policeman" line, somewhat famous from the film, wasn't from the book, either.) The most notable alteration is that Dr. No is made a member of SPECTRE, not yet in existence in the book, and he has metal hands instead of pinchers. Bond's escape through the tunnel takes the place of the obstacle course of death. While the scalding water that cascades across the crawling Bond in the tunnel was a nod to the book, the logic of its inclusion in the film is curious.

---

[136] While books can get away with long monologues, films typically cannot, and so Dr. No's long speech on his history was greatly shortened.

While the book ended with Bond dispatching the giant squid and Dr. No in short order, the movie's version, where Bond foils Dr. No's plans, is arguably better.[137] So, in that sense, the film has a greater sense of urgency and stakes even if we lose Bond's terrible ordeal along the way. It also allows for Dr. No to be a physical threat to Bond, whereas in the book, he was only an intellectual threat. In many ways, the climax of the *Dr. No* movie is a precursor to more fantastic versions of the same—Bond infiltrates the base to stop the bad guy. If viewed out of order, *Dr. No*'s ending may not seem that grand compared to its sequels, but during its 1962 premiere, Bond's duel with Dr. No on the sinking platform was a very exciting scene.[138] Lastly, the book and the movie have different end caps. The book had a running joke about Bond owing Honey "slave time," while the movie has Bond untethering he and Honey's raft from Leiter's rescue boat so that he and Honey can have some alone time.

Lucky for us, *Dr. No* was a success, though maybe not of the magnitude that some imply. The film ended its first theatrical run with a gross of around $6 million versus its $1 million budget, which made it profitable, but it wasn't a financial juggernaut, nor was it a critical darling. Besides, Broccoli and Saltzman had ideas of a long running Bond franchise from the onset. Therefore, one could argue the film was successful enough to warrant the desired sequels, which would fortunately improve upon the formula as time went on.

---

[137] It's probably for the best the squid got the ax, as it may have given the audience outlandish expectations for the series from the get-go. Also, even Disney's big budget *20,000 Leagues Under the Sea* had difficulty crafting a convincing giant squid and had to obscure theirs behind a rainstorm.

[138] In some ways, of all the films, *Dr. No* was shortchanged due to its lower budget, even if Ken Adam pulled off a lot of expensive-looking sets. On the other hand, the producers also felt that it might be the easiest one to budget since most of it was confined to an island. If any of the Bond films deserve a remake today, it's *Dr No*.

GOLDFINGER

PUBLICATION DATE:
March 23, 1959
ORIGINAL PAGE LENGTH:
318pp.
PUBLISHER: Jonathan Cape

It is often said that *Goldfinger* set the gold-standard for James Bond movies, beginning with an exciting pre-title scene—typically unrelated to the rest of the film—followed by a credit sequence of scantily clad women dancing to the title song in a way that tied in with the film's overall motif. Other staples included a grandiose villain accompanied by a uniquely enhanced henchman. Bond should also play some kind of game with the villain—in this case, golf with Goldfinger. That there should be a secondary or supporting "Bond girl" in addition to the main one was established via Jill Masterson. Usually, the secondary Bond girls met grisly ends, and none's demise was more memorable than the golden girl. Bond being captured, then dining with the villain was another staple (even though, technically, it had been established in *Dr. No*.) The villain staging an elaborate death trap for Bond to escape was another must. Lastly was both a grand climax and something akin to the pre-credit scene in the sense that there would be one last, unexpected scrape for Bond before the end credits rolled. And, prior to the credits rolling, Bond always got the girl.[139]

Goldfinger hit those all-important notes not only for the first time, but in spades at that. As the quintessential Bond film, it's quite interesting to compare it to its source material. As is usually the case, in some regards the book was better—Bond and Goldfinger's fascinating dialogue—and in others, the movie improved upon the source material—in the book, Goldfinger really is crazy enough to try and cart away all of Fort Knox's gold instead of irradiating it.

WRITING *GOLDFINGER*

As usual, the bulk of *Goldfinger* was written in the early winter months of 1958 and released a little over a year later in March of 1959. Its first draft, entitled "The Richest Man in the World" and running 270 pages, was Fleming's longest yet. While Fleming had to resort to an abandoned teleplay to craft *Dr. No*, *Goldfinger* was a wholly original Bond adventure apart from one early scene. Around this same time, Fleming had been asked about the possibility of a James Bond TV series which he drafted up a few ideas for. When said television series amounted to naught, he turned the teleplay ideas into James Bond short stories, resulting in the collection entitled *For Your Eyes Only*.[140] In the case of *Goldfinger*, Fleming managed to use one of the scraped episode scenarios as the jumping off point for a whole novel, and one of his longest ones at that. The scenario in question is Bond catching Goldfinger cheating at cards.

---

[139] Or at least up until *Quantum of Solace* in 2008.

[140] The TV series was briefly discussed on page 29 and will be covered more thoroughly in Volume II regarding *For Your Eyes Only*.

As to the title character, Fleming had always rather innocently named characters after people he knew. In this case, he named one after someone he didn't know personally and paid the price. There was a prominent architect by the name of Ernő Goldfinger who, upon finding out about the novel, threatened Fleming with a lawsuit, which was settled out of court. How the matter was settled is unknown, and in either case, Fleming had always been fascinated with gold and wanted a villain who was as well.[141] (Fleming had a gold-plated typewriter himself.) As a further aside, the same 1955 INTERPOL conference that helped birth *From Russia, with Love* featured a report on the magnitude of gold smuggling which had also intrigued Fleming. As usual, other real-life events triggered ideas for the story, such as a showgirl who died from skin asphyxiation when she covered herself in body paint. Bond and Goldfinger's game of golf was inspired by Fleming's playing in the June 1957 Bowmaker Pro-Am golf tournament at the Berkshire Golf Club.

Goldfinger was well-received by Fleming's colleagues and beta-readers like William Plomer, who considered it one of his best Bond stories and who even suggested a Pussy Galore spinoff.[142] By then, the Bond books had gained considerable traction and *Goldfinger* placed quite easily on best-seller lists. It even garnered an appearance by Fleming on *The Bookman*, a British TV show, and he had a book signing at Harrods.

---

[141] Fleming for certain disliked Erno Goldfinger, though, because he had destroyed many Victorian era buildings that Fleming loved, replacing them with structures with modernistic designs. As for a further interesting coincidence, Fleming's partner in the June 1957 Bowmaker Pro-Am golf tournament also disliked Goldfinger and he was apparently a topic of discussion between the two during the game.

[142] Maybe I'm putting words in his mouth, so in the interest of being accurate, he wrote, "Pussy is a real wit – I should like to read a whole book about her." [Fleming, *Man with the Golden Typewriter*, p.199.]

Although Fleming considered *Goldfinger* to have been his easiest Bond book to write, he lamented to William Plomer that it might be "the last full length folio on Bond ... Though I may be able to think up some episodes for him in the future, I shall never be able to give him 70,000 words again."[143] While Fleming would next cobble together a book out of short stories, that being *For Your Eyes Only*, he would eventually go on to write and publish four more full-length Bond novels.

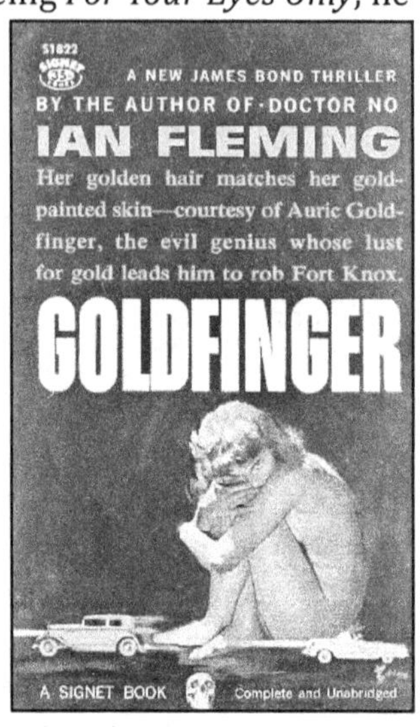

READING *GOLDFINGER*

While the previous books maintained a healthy continuity in the sense that we often opened on Bond still recovering and reflecting upon his last adventure, *Goldfinger* finds Bond on the way home from a mission we didn't see. Although in the eventual film we would witness Bond's Latin American mission firsthand, here we find Bond thinking about the assignment after the fact, having just killed a Mexican drug lord and blown up his poppy field. Unlike Connery's character, Fleming's Bond is a bit down after the killing. That's why when Bond finds himself in Miami on a layover, he decides to get stinking drunk as he hasn't gotten drunk in ages, according to Bond's inner monologue.

Bond's planned night of debauchery is interrupted by an old connection named Mr. Du Pont, a minor supporting player from *Casino Royale* who reminds Bond that they played baccarat together. DuPont hopes that Bond can help him expose his nemesis, Auric Goldfinger, who he suspects of constantly cheating at cards. If Bond can prove

143 Pearson, *The Life of Ian Fleming*, p.361, p.369.

that Goldfinger is a cheater, DuPont will pay him $10,000. While initially this plot device might seem a little too repetitive of *Moonraker*, where Bond catches Drax cheating at cards, it amounts to an amusing scene and a great way to introduce the titular villain. Compared to the films, being privy to Bond's inner monologue is amusing when reading the books, especially regarding his first meeting with Goldfinger. Specifically, Bond describes Goldfinger as looking as though he was cobbled together from the body parts of different people. Being short, Bond doesn't trust Goldfinger since, by Bond's reasoning, short men like Hitler and Napoleon always cause trouble in the world. The card game is enough like the movie's that it's not worth going over other than to say that it's interesting to see it play out via Fleming's prose. Also, Bond sees to it that Jill Masterson leaves the hotel with him so that she is safe and forces Goldfinger to book them both passage out of Miami. Bond even gives Jill the $10,000 paid to him by DuPont to make sure that she's safe.

Back in London, Fleming adds another aspect of himself to Bond in that he is writing a book, or rather a government manual, on hand-to-hand combat. Bond's burgeoning book is interrupted when he's assigned the task of investigating Goldfinger on suspicions of gold smuggling.[144] (Eventually, Goldfinger will be revealed to be the treasurer of SMERSH, an aspect cast aside for the film version of the character.[145]) Interestingly, Bond uses a device called the "Identicast" to help identify Goldfinger, which would turn up in 1981's *For Your Eyes Only* even if it didn't in 1964's *Goldfinger*.

---

[144] As was the case with Drax in *Moonraker*, M knows Goldfinger from the Blades Club, which he is said to visit when in England.

[145] It's interesting they didn't try to make him an agent of SPECTRE in the film as they had done with Dr. No and Rosa Kleb. This makes the cinematic version of Goldfinger a rare animal in that he was the only foe Connery's Bond faced that wasn't linked in some way to SPECTRE.

The "Identicast" eventually leads Bond to deduct that the best way to catch Goldfinger is when he's out playing golf, and only Fleming could make a golf game suspenseful and entertaining. Bond's bridge game against Drax in the third 007 novel had been entertaining in its own right, but it was this golf game that really cemented the tradition of Bond competing against the villain. Notably, Oddjob does not serve as caddy in the book, and Bond needs to win the game to impress Goldfinger in the hope that he might recruit him into his crime syndicate. The book has an additional scene where, after the golf game, Goldfinger invites Bond over to his estate for dinner. As Oddjob was mostly absent from the golf game, in the book, this sequence serves to showcase Oddjob and his deadly skills.

Goldfinger states that he calls him Oddjob because that's what he does for him: odd jobs. For once, it's the book version of the character that's more far-out than its film counterpart. While we see Oddjob crush a golf ball in the movie, the only implication is that he's spectacularly strong. In the book, his hands are deformed in the sense that they are extremely hard, like solid bone. This Oddjob is also capable of martial arts with a wide spectrum of agility. And, just when I thought the hat would turn out to be an invention of the film, it features in the book in full force as well. Furthermore, Bond is impressed with Oddjob, admiring him to the extent that he wants to include him in his hand-to-hand combat manual. (Remember, in the book, Oddjob had yet to kill either of the Masterson sisters as far as Bond knows.)

Dinner at Goldfinger's is mostly a ruse. As soon as Bond arrives, Goldfinger must leave on an emergency business errand, which he assures 007 won't last more than thirty minutes. Although Bond smells a trap, he can't pass up the opportunity to snoop through the house where he eventually discovers a camera filming his movements. Bond exposes the film—remember this is the 1950s—and makes it look as though Goldfinger's pet cat is the culprit behind the mangled footage. When Goldfinger returns home, he offers the cat to Oddjob for dinner—Goldfinger's way of implying to Bond that the cat trick didn't work and that he's onto him.

The dinner that follows is a fine scene, though as a writer, I can see how it would have been difficult to include without slowing the film's pace. (That's why it was more or less combined into the golf scene.) Not only is Goldfinger one of the best onscreen villains, he has a marvelous presence on the page as well. He and Bond's verbal sparring match over dinner is another sheer delight from Fleming. It's always nice to see an author progress in their art form, and Fleming's dinner between 007 and Goldfinger showcases his best dialogue yet.

The novel progresses similarly to the film, with Bond trailing Goldfinger and running into Tilly Masterson. Since Bond lacks a gadget-laden car, he fakes a fender bender with Tilly to get her off the road and out of his way. Through Tilly, we eventually learn of Jill's fate and then some. In the movie, we assume Jill was the only girl that Goldfinger ever painted gold. In the book, it's revealed to be a sexual fetish Goldfinger exposes all his women to, and he has a new one every month. None of them die, as they aren't painted entirely, but with Jill, he purposely didn't leave a skin patch so that she would suffocate to death.

Just as there's no golden girl for Bond to lay eyes on in the book, there's also no laser to threaten him with. Instead, Bond is placed spread eagle on a table with a buzzsaw—probably more painful than a laser though not as fantastic. Odder yet, for those only familiar with the film, Tilly is still alive but in a state of hypnosis, with Goldfinger using her as leverage against Bond. Goldfinger is not so stupid as to tell Bond if he talks, he can go. He makes the reasonable proposition, for a deranged villain at least, that if Bond talks, he will give him and Tilly a pill that will provide a painless death. If not, Bond will die in "one long scream" as Goldfinger puts it, and Tilly will be given to Oddjob. (Nor is there the infamous, "No, I expect you to die," line, which was added by screenwriters.)

Instead of Bond striking a bargain with Goldfinger as in the movie, Bond thinks himself dead meat in the book and passes out. He awakens on a plane as in the film, but not to the beautiful visage of Pussy Galore, who, like Honey Rider before her, will make a rather late entrance into the story later. Initially, Bond thinks he might be in Heaven, and humorously muses as to whether all his dead girlfriends will get along together, thinking of Vesper Lynd and the Masterson sisters.[146]

As it turns out, Bond's gamble paid off, and Goldfinger admires him enough to enlist him in his organization after all. Specifically, Goldfinger wants Bond and Tilly to work for him on Operation Grand Slam. This is where the book differs the most from its adaptation, with Tilly living on to be a major character. As odd as it sounds, she and Bond are to serve as Goldfinger's secretaries in the operation's planning stages, which involves a conglomerate of gangsters. Later, when Bond reads a memo of the invited gangsters, he sees the old Spangled Mob from *Diamonds Are Forever* listed and also someone called Pussy Galore,

[146] Bond is quite fond of Jill Masterson in the book compared to the film, where he barely got to know her.

which intrigues him.[147] Pussy's not a pilot in the book, but, appropriately, a cat burglar with an all-female gang. In Goldfinger's words, they are a "lesbian organization" called "The Cement Mixers." Neither are Pussy, or Tilly, for that matter, blondes and both have black hair. Furthermore, Tilly is a lesbian as well and only has eyes for Pussy Galore, so there is no romance between Tilly and Bond for those wondering.

In place of the laser, Goldfinger plans to use a small, "clean" atomic warhead to breach Fort Knox. Nor is there any secret plan to irradiate the gold and leave it there—this Goldfinger is crazy enough to try and remove all of Fort Knox's gold for himself. As opposed to gas in the air as in the film, Goldfinger plans to poison the water supply of Fort Knox. And, just when I thought Felix Leiter was added to the film version as he was for *Dr. No*, towards the end of the book, Leiter comes to the rescue. (You could say Bond sends him a message in a bottle asking for aid via Pinkerton's.) At Fort Knox, Leiter shows up with the cavalry to interrupt Operation Grand Slam. Notably, we never get inside Fort Knox, and Goldfinger goes on the run. Nor does Bond kill Oddjob during this sequence, and instead, this is where Oddjob finally gets Tilly with his deadly hat.

Although I assumed the airplane ending was something tacked onto the film, it comes from the book, too. At the airport, Bond gets drugged and awakens on a plane sitting next to Oddjob. Goldfinger and Pussy Galore are there, too, with the latter having a sudden change of heart and slipping notes to Bond that she is on his side. Interestingly, the final set piece sees Oddjob sucked through the depressurized window, not Goldfinger, who Bond fights and strangles to death while the plane is still in midair. The novel concludes with Bond and Pussy alive and well and

---

[147] This is what we would today call a continuity "Easter Egg" and there's no pay off or impact on the plot whereas the Spangled Mob is concerned.

recuperating in a hotel room, where Bond tells Pussy she needs some T.L.C.—tender love and care.

Ultimately, *Goldfinger* might well be the book where Fleming managed to combine his *From Russia, with Love*-like prose with the more adventurous formula of *Dr. No*. Overall, I think the film is a better iteration of *Goldfinger* in that it's less convoluted than the book. The only way in which the book betters the movie is in the relationship between Bond and Goldfinger as two opponents who both despise yet respect one another's abilities. Bond notes early on that if Goldfinger were merely smuggling gold, he would be so impressed with him that he would let him go. Likewise, in the final scene aboard the plane, Goldfinger tells Bond he will adhere to his last requests out of respect for him having been a worthy opponent.

If there's any qualms to be had with the book, it's Bond's relationship with Pussy. While their interactions are always welcome, and Pussy intrigues in every scene she's in, she gets shortchanged due to a lack of… should we call it page-time instead of screentime? She's a knockout of a character, and her last-minute save of Bond makes for a great surprise, but the movie version correctly afforded her more attention and worked better narratively. Still, maybe Fleming gave her more mystique by having her presence being somewhat limited compared to her predecessors.[148]

---

[148] As a slight recompense, Anthony Horowitz featured Pussy Galore in the first act of *Trigger Mortis*, which utilized an unfinished story by

DEVELOPING EON's *GOLDFINGER*

Ironically, what is considered the Bond film that set the standard for the whole series was considered difficult to adapt from its source material by Richard Maibaum, who completed his first treatment for *Goldfinger* before *From Russia with Love* had even hit theaters on May 19, 1963. Removing SMERSH from the equation created several plot holes in terms of Auric Goldfinger's motivations.[149] Maibaum also felt Bond meeting Goldfinger by coincidence before being assigned to him was a bit too much.[150] Maibaum was also incensed that Jill Masterson's dead body, painted in gold, wasn't shown in the book as Bond only heard about it through dialogue with Tilly. On the note of Tilly, Maibaum also pointed out that there wasn't enough "romance" in the book, since the romance, if it could be called that, with Pussy Galore doesn't happen until the last pages.

One thing Maibaum did appreciate about *Goldfinger* was that it had started with Bond fresh off of an assignment unrelated to the book's main storyline. In that vein, Maibaum kept the idea of an opening scene somewhere in Latin America. His first crack at it is remarkably similar to the finished product aside from Felix Leiter popping up in the cantina. Maibaum also comes up with a fairly funny line regarding Bond's handgun, even if the finished film's version is better. If you'll recall, the dancer, Bonita, asks Bond why he carries a gun and he replies that he has "a slight inferiority complex." In this treatment, Bond quips that he carries the gun for sentimental reasons: it was his grandmother's.

Fleming and is, presumably, canon and in continuity with Fleming's works, unlike the other Bond continuation novels.

[149] However, why he couldn't be working for SPECTRE I don't know.

[150] That said, among Bond and Goldfinger's many conversations was one on the nature of coincidence, happenstance, and "enemy action," as Goldfinger called it.

Upon arrival in Miami, Bond's flight is delayed and so he wishes to spend the evening getting drunk for the first time in years. Like the book, but uncharacteristic for Connery's Bond at this point, 007 is remorseful over the man he killed in Mexico—hence wanting to get falling-down drunk. Though faithful to the novel, it's good this idea was eventually dropped. Soon after, the DuPont character approaches Bond, recognizing him from a French casino they gambled at years before.[151] Despite Maibaum's aversion to coincidence, Bond and Goldfinger's first meeting still comes as such. In fact, the treatment sticks to the novel right down to Goldfinger claiming to have Agoraphobia, a fear of open spaces, hence why he has to sit facing the hotel. (If Goldfinger faces the hotel, then DuPont must have his back to it, enabling Jill Masterson to spy on DuPont.)

After discovering the ruse, Bond makes Goldfinger pay DuPont interest, then takes Jill away on the train. And while initially it appears she escapes her onscreen fate, this isn't so. Back in London, Bond is working the nightshift at Mi6 while also compiling his hand-to-hand combat manual. In this case, he makes a flirty demonstration of it for Moneypenny before getting a call from Jill asking him to come to her apartment—apparently she moved to London with Bond. When Bond arrives there, he finds the dead Jill painted gold. From this point, Maibaum's outline better resembles the film, including a visit with Colonel Smithers and a trip to Q Branch for a tricked-out Aston Martin DB III, although all of the touted gadgets curiously seem to go unused in this treatment. One gadget Bond gets to use is a car phone, which M calls Bond on and informs him that Jill was not found painted gold, contrary to his report.

I have to commend Maibaum for doing something Fleming didn't. During the golf game, Bond asks Goldfinger

---

[151] Again, in the novel, this was a reference to *Casino Royale* which Mr. DuPont and his wife both appeared in.

how his agoraphobia is, considering golf is a game played in wide open spaces. The golf game isn't different enough to warrant much commentary, but as in the book, it does result in Bond getting invited over to Goldfinger's for dinner. There, Goldfinger admits he'd like to hire Bond right away (just as Bond hoped) as opposed to the novel. When Goldfinger leaves on emergency business, Bond snoops around and notably finds a statue of a golden woman in his bedroom. Afterwards, things are similar to the novel, Oddjob eating the cat and all.

Later, and despite having plenty of gadgets, Bond still fakes a fender bender to get Tilly Masterson's attention. As in the film and the source material, Bond eventually reunites with Tilly as she attempts to assassinate Goldfinger. As in the novel, she informs him of Goldfinger's practice of painting his women gold as a fetish, though it wasn't lethal until Jill. Tilly also reveals it was she who washed the gold paint from Jill's body, explaining why her body was found in a clean state by the authorities.

As the treatment progresses, Maibaum keeps a great line from the novel about the third meeting being "enemy action" but swaps the buzzsaw for a laser he had read about in *LIFE*. And yes, Tilly is still alive at this point as in the book, but the "No, I expect you die" line isn't present yet. Also as in the literary version, Bond and Tilly are forced to work as accomplices for Goldfinger in New York. Pussy Galore stays a mobster and Tilly is still implied to be a lesbian. (When Bond kisses her, she becomes furious and tells him she dislikes men.) Bond has Tilly type up a message for Felix Leiter, sight unseen in this version since the Miami airport bit. (It also explains why Maibaum inserted Leiter into the pre-credit scene, so Leiter won't come out of nowhere as he does in the novel.) The book features a scene of Goldfinger's plane flying over Fort Knox and being told over the radio that it's forbidden airspace. In the book, Goldfinger says he is location scouting for Paramount Pictures, while the treatment naturally rephrases it to become United Artists.

The treatment proceeds almost exactly like the novel, which means no fight inside of Fort Knox. Like the book, Bond's plane is hijacked by Goldfinger, Pussy, Oddjob, and one of the gangsters. Said gangster just happened to work for SMERSH in the past and recognizes Bond as the 00 agent that he is, and so Goldfinger tells Bond he wants to keep him alive as a valuable hostage. As opposed to shooting out the window of the plane, Bond uses a screwdriver to break the window—much less exciting, obviously. And, yes, Pussy only switches sides at the last minute here as well.

When providing notes on how to improve the logic of the treatments to follow, Maibaum ingeniously pointed out that poisoning the water supply necessitated that all the citizens of Fort Knox would need to drink water at the same time to lose consciousness simultaneously. As such, gas sprayed in the air was a more logical option. Therefore, exit Pussy Galore the mobster and enter Pussy Galore the pilot, along with her flying circus, in the next treatment.[152]

The second, shorter treatment is much like the first, only Bond is no longer remorseful about the man he killed in the pre-credit scene. (For that matter, I'm not sure if the previous treatment ever resolved that minor story thread, either.) In this one, Jill Masterson catches Bond's eye first as he observes her, Goldfinger, and DuPont from a distance. Later, Bond just happens to see Jill helping Goldfinger cheat—there is no connection between Bond and DuPont and the fateful sequence of events is instigated due to Bond's interest in Jill. In simplifying the story, Maibaum finally decides to do away with poor old Tilly, and she suffers Oddjob's hat trick for the first time early on. As for other changes, Bond poses as an underworld operative/gangster, which lends more naturally to Goldfinger recruiting him. Along those same lines, it also

---

[152] On the note of Pussy's somewhat troublesome first name, Kitty Galore was considered as an alternative. Fleming rightly balked and helped convince the producers to keep her rightful first name.

appears to Oddjob as though Bond saves Goldfinger's life when he stops Tilly from assassinating him.

New York is finally out for the Operation Grand Slam conference and Kentucky is in. And as stated before, Pussy is now the aerial delivery agent for the gas, while Bond is tasked with driving a tank through the front gate of Fort Knox. Maibaum also introduces his ingenious idea to irradiate Fort Knox as a way of devaluing the U.S. gold supply. The ending is closer to the final film aside from Bond driving the tank through Fort Knox. Nor is there a ruse regarding the plane at the very end. During the final battle, Goldfinger takes 007 hostage when he retreats Fort Knox as its defended by the U.S. army. Goldfinger commandeers a plane bound for Cuba with 007 in tow, the fight aboard the plane occurs, and it all ends with Bond promising to give Pussy some T.L.C. in keeping with the novel's dialogue.

The screenplay version follows the second treatment for the most part but deviates from the book by having Bond bed Tilly—a pretty big departure. Tilly sneaks out of bed to go assassinate Goldfinger and Bond follows. As for other interesting asides, Pussy Galore dons the golden paint at one point and does a dance for the mobsters as entertainment. Nor does Goldfinger gas the gangsters in this version and they are present during the final assault at Fort Knox. Towards the end, Goldfinger knocks out Bond with the aid of Pussy and takes 007 to the escape plane. During the same sequence, Bond explains to Pussy that the real nerve gas was supposed to have been lethal. Had it not been switched out, Pussy would've become a mass murderer. Enraged by this revelation, Pussy switches sides and goes against Goldfinger at the last second. Pussy also manages to land the plane, although she and Bond jump out of it before it explodes. They are promptly picked up by Leiter, who drives them off to a hotel that he reserved for them ten minutes earlier, anticipating Bond's usual behavior, thus ending on a joke.

Paul Dehn was brought in to work on the next script, which oddly begins with Bond diving under the cover of a dead dog instead of a pigeon as in the film. In this script we also would've seen M playing bridge at his club, The Blades, which featured prominently in the *Moonraker* novel. Dehn has a great handle on M, as evidenced by a new scene taking place in Bond's office. As 007 is briefed on Goldfinger by a colleague, Bond throws knives at a target on his door. In comes M without knocking and a knife sails past his head. "I want you to report to Q right away. You don't deserve it, but we're lending you a car. And making a small deduction from your salary," M says while glaring at the knife embedded in the wall.[153] Dehn also envisions a totally different set of gags for Q Branch, with fire trucks spewing fire instead of water from their hoses and so on.

This is also the first script to do away with the idea of Bond posing as a gangster. Instead, as in the film, Goldfinger simply thinks that with Bond alive, he will have less interference from the Secret Service. It appears that Dehn may have originated a variation of the "No, I expect you to die" line, which is slightly different in his script, though similar in spirit. (On that note, Dehn excelled at his dialogue overall.)

When Bond wakes up on the airplane, Goldfinger and Oddjob are there, too. Bond's first meeting with Pussy Galore occurs when he gets too close to her cockpit, and she does some judo moves on him. This causes Oddjob to laugh hysterically, and Pussy tells Goldfinger that she'll fly him to hell and back, but passengers better stay the hell away from her cockpit. Of course, there's only room for so many one-liners and zingers before they get out of hand, but Dehn wrote great dialogue, and it's too bad some of it went unutilized. For instance, when Goldfinger tells Pussy to keep up appearances with Bond for the sake of his CIA friends watching from afar, he tells her to take his arm

---

[153] Feutry, *Scripting 007*, p.140.

without breaking it if possible. (Regarding Pussy, her being a lesbian is downplayed greatly in this script.)

In this script we also finally get inside of Fort Knox. In *The James Bond Archives* by Paul Duncan, *Goldfinger* director Guy Hamilton spoke on the nature of the book's climax versus the film's, stating, "Fleming let us down in the book, because all the villains get as far as Fort Knox but they all get arrested outside [of it at the] end of story. You can't do that in a movie." Likewise, this is also the first draft where Bond fights and kills Oddjob inside of Fort Knox.

Notably, Pussy's change of heart comes about due to what ended up being a deleted scene on the helicopter between her and Goldfinger. As they escape the chaos of Fort Knox, Pussy states that she thought the knockout gas was supposed to last for 48 hours. Goldfinger admits to her that he deceived her, and that it was actually supposed to be lethal gas before a double agent switched it. When she angrily says that she and her flying circus would've murdered close to 60,000 people, Goldfinger responds that traffic accidents kill that many people every year, which is also a line from the book. As for a rather convoluted twist, since in this version it couldn't have been Pussy to switch the canisters, it turns out that Felix Leiter had a double agent in Pussy's flying circus all along.

Dehn's original closer was similar to an aborted final shot for *From Russia with Love,* where Bond was to break the fourth wall by looking directly into the camera and acknowledging the audience. In this case, Dehn wanted to fake out the audience via a cutaway shot from the plane going down to a couple of gurneys bearing corpses, the immediate implication being that Bond and Pussy bit the dust. However, it becomes clear that it's actually Oddjob and Goldfinger on the gurneys, and the camera would pan up to reveal Bond alive, looking into the camera and stating, "We made it." A red theater curtain was to then fall over Bond and Pussy as they begin to kiss, really breaking the fourth wall since the red curtain comes out of nowhere.

When Maibaum critiqued Dehn's script, he naturally pointed out that it was far too fantastical, even if he did like plenty of Dehn's changes. Regarding the comedic bits, Maibaum remarked that it seemed more like the script was written for Bob Hope and Bing Crosby than Sean Connery. As a fix to Dehn's last shot, Maibaum suggested that Bond and Pussy could escape the plane sharing a parachute and potentially, in his parlance, be "screwing" in midair.[154]

Connery had strong feelings regarding Dehn's script, too. He shared Maibaum's opinion that it was too cutesy and also felt that there needed to be more of a connection between Bond and Pussy Galore. Ultimately, Maibaum would revise Dehn's script, striking a proper balance between Dehn's clever humor and the seriousness of the previous two Bond movies.[155]

---

[154] While Bond may not have had coitus in the clouds with Pussy Galore, he appeared to be having underwater sex with Domino in the next film, 1965's *Thunderball*.

[155] Aside from differing dialogue, the only thing that really stands out to me about the final screenplay was that during the climax, it has a bit where Bond confronts Oddjob while driving a forklift in Fort Knox, which couldn't help but remind me of the final scene in *Aliens*. And, true to Maibaum's comment in his letter, the final shots were to have been of Bond and Pussy kissing in midair as their parachute floats towards the ground.

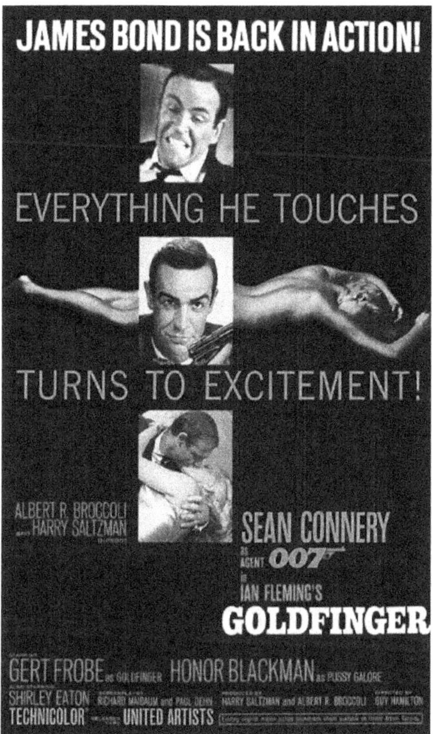

RELEASE DATE:
September 1964 (UK)
December 1964 (US)
RUNTIME: 110 Minutes
DIRECTOR:
Guy Hamilton
PRODUCERS:
Albert R. Broccoli
& Harry Saltzman
SCREENPLAY: Richard Maibaum & Paul Dehn
MUSIC: John Barry
CAST: Sean Connery (James Bond) Honor Blackman (Pussy Galore) Gert Fröbe (Auric Goldfinger) Shirley Eaton (Jill Masterson) Harold Sakata (Oddjob) Cec Linder (Felix Leiter) Bernard Lee (M) Lois Maxwell (Moneypenny) Desmond Llewelyn (Q)

WATCHING *GOLDFINGER* (1964)

Technically, *From Russia with Love* did feature a pre-credit sequence. However, like its source material, it was simply a means of introducing audiences to the villains before Bond himself. It was also a relatively simple scene. *Goldfinger*, by comparison, throws a lot at the audience in the first few minutes, with explosions, clever fisticuffs, plus some great visual gags and one-liners. The fact that Bond sees his attacker in a reflection of his deceptive lover's eye and lets her take the blow meant for him was no doubt shocking for audiences of the time. Bond's means of dispatching his attacker through electrocution was both clever and also a way, perhaps, of foreshadowing Oddjob's death later.

Though inspired by Bond's unseen mission from the book, Bond's Latin American adventure has nothing to do with the rest of the film's story, making it its own self-contained mini-movie in a way.[156] Another important aspect of *Goldfinger* is its amazing title song by Shirley Bassey, which is accompanied by Maurice Binder's title sequence of golden girls. (*From Russia with Love* had also rolled its credits after a pre-title sequence, but it offered only an instrumental version of the title song with credits rather simplistically projected onto a belly dancer.)

As to how the final film compares to the book, Bond's chance meeting with Goldfinger thanks to DuPont is simply retrofitted to become M giving Bond a message via Felix Leiter that he wants Goldfinger investigated. Nor does Bond know Simmons, the replacement character for DuPont. Though visually striking and iconic today, some have felt Jill's golden death presented something of a plot hole because, why wouldn't Goldfinger have killed Jill and Bond both? (Why Oddjob doesn't kill Bond in the movie is better explained in the book, as it was Goldfinger's way of warning and taunting Bond at the same time.) However, even if the sequence of events may have puzzled a few audience members, it was still worth it to have Bond on hand to witness Jill's fate for himself.

As for other minor differences, Bond meets with Colonel Smithers one-on-one in the book, but M joins the duo for dinner in the film. The movie condenses and speeds up things nicely after the golf game, removing Bond's visit to Goldfinger's mansion and killing Tilly Masterson early on. Frankly, Tilly would have bogged the story down had she

---

[156] *Thunderball* would follow this model with another action sequence totally unrelated to main storyline. However, from *You Only Live Twice* through *The Spy Who Loved Me*, the pre-title scenes would tie into the main story. It wasn't until 1981's *For Your Eyes Only* that a pre-title scene with absolutely nothing to do with the rest of the film would finally resurface. More often than not though, the pre-title scenes typically tie into the main storyline in some minor way.

survived. Plus, alluding to Pussy being a lesbian was one thing for movies of the time, but for Tilly to make eyes and flirt with Pussy onscreen would've pushed the envelope for 1960s-era audiences. The line, "You can turn off the charm, I'm immune," is ultimately the only hint Pussy's not into men. Pussy shows up halfway through the film, earlier than she does in the book, and is afforded much more attention than her literary counterpart overall.

Bond and Pussy's new roles in the film versus the book were also more logical. Making Bond Goldfinger's prisoner rather than his secretary also simplified things. And while Pussy Galore the mob boss was certainly interesting, Pussy Galore the pilot made more sense. Not only did it enable a better way to knock out the population of Fort Knox via aerial nerve gas, but it also gave Pussy a more logical reason to be on the plane at the end. Furthermore, Goldfinger gasses the mob in the movie anyways, which would have been further complicated had Pussy remained a mob boss.

Speaking of the mobsters, the scene where Goldfinger kills them all was quite shocking for audiences.[157] Like Oddjob's sparing of Bond earlier, the mass murder puzzled a few audience members who asked why Goldfinger went to all the trouble to explain his grandiose plan to the mobsters if he was just going to kill them anyways. From a story perspective, the scene was necessary so that both Bond and the audience could finally learn what Goldfinger was up to. From a psychological perspective within the logic of the film itself, one could argue that Goldfinger wanted to boast of his genius in front of colleagues who could actually appreciate the beauty of his plan, even if he was going to kill them. Lastly, it's important to remember that the gangsters had already all done their jobs for Goldfinger and were therefore expendable.

---

[157] As an aside, most of the gangsters in the movie have the same names from the book apart from the Spangled Mob, which doesn't appear, and a few others.

The film's biggest improvement over its source material is easily Goldfinger's plot to irradiate Fort Knox. Ironically, in the book, Goldfinger planned to use a clean bomb on Fort Knox, but the bomb of the movie is extra dirty so that the gold will be untouchable for years to come. This new scheme also enables a peek inside of Fort Knox via Ken Adam's amazing set. (The producers wanted a "cathedral of gold" and Ken Adam delivered.)

The film naturally also has a great deal more action than the book, with the biggest addition being the car chase through the woods outside Auric Enterprises in the Aston Martin DB5. Though some fans would come to resent Bond's over-reliance on gadgets in the future, you can't argue that the gadget-enhanced DB5 was a big factor in *Goldfinger*'s success, not to mention 007's enduring popularity for decades to come. The "No, I expect you to die" line was another great addition that wouldn't have been possible in the book and it's become one of the great lines of cinema. When Bond mentions Operation Grand Slam to save his life, Goldfinger tells Bond, "You are worth more to me alive." Following that, one of his men promptly shoots Bond at point-blank range, making for a great fake-out as well. Like all Bond films, the film's logic sometimes suffers for the sake of cool ideas, but the pacing is perfect.

Goldfinger was not only a financial juggernaut, it also became a cultural phenomenon.[158] Sadly, Ian Fleming passed away roughly a month before the film premiered. Fleming had suffered a heart attack on August 11, 1964, and died the next day. Ever the British gentleman, his last recorded words were to his ambulance drivers, to whom he quipped, "I am sorry to trouble you chaps. I don't know how you get along so fast with the traffic on the roads these days."[159]

---

[158] It recouped its budget in only two weeks and went on to gross $46 million worldwide, and then added even more numbers to its total when it was double billed with *Dr. No* for a 1966 rerelease.
[159] Lycett, *Ian Fleming*, p.443.

The Return of Goldfinger

Considering the popularity of 1964's *Goldfinger*, it should come as no surprise that the title character almost returned in a sequel. Though discussed only briefly in the chapter devoted to *Diamonds Are Forever*, I thought it more pertinent to include the details of Goldfinger's axed return here. Some sources have implied that Goldfinger's return was planned as early as *OHMSS*. Per this theory, the ending of *OHMSS* was actually supposed to be the beginning of *Diamonds Are Forever*, already being developed. While one might expect the potential pre-credits scene to have Blofeld assassinating Tracy Bond, that's not who would do it. It was originally to be Auric Goldfinger's twin brother out for revenge! During production of *OHMSS* it became apparent that George Lazenby may not return for another Bond epic. And so, the planned pre-credit scene for *Diamonds* became the new, impactful epilogue of *OHMSS*. Or so the story goes.

However, that was likely just a disambiguation of the facts.[160] While the twin of Goldfinger would be considered for *Diamonds Are Forever*, this didn't happen until well into that film's developmental process. Like the creation of Willard Whyte, it was Cubby Broccoli's dream about Howard Hughes that inspired Richard Maibaum to insert Goldfinger's brother into the script. The idea was twofold. One was that if Cubby wanted a mysterious millionaire character in the story, why not make it Goldfinger's twin? And, if the first Goldfinger was obsessed with gold, this one could be obsessed with diamonds. Actually, the idea might have been threefold instead of twofold. With Sean Connery's return only being hoped for and not a certainty, having Gert Fröbe return as Goldfinger's twin brother would at least give audiences another returning actor other than Bernard Lee and Lois Maxwell.

---

[160] The rumor may have also stemmed from a discarded story element of *OHMSS* which would have revealed that Blofeld and the dearly departed Goldfinger were half-brothers.

Interestingly, Goldfinger #2 didn't replace Blofeld as the main villain of *Diamonds Are Forever* and instead would form an uneasy alliance with Bond to take down Blofeld. Maibaum's treatment had Goldfinger's brother as a powerful, Swedish shipping magnate, known under the alias of Adamas Sten.[161] Bond seeks out Sten in relation to stolen diamonds in Thailand, and is shocked to see that Sten is obviously Goldfinger's twin brother. Sten, however, either feigns ignorance as to who Bond is or just doesn't know what he looks like. In any case, Sten has his own Oddjob-like henchman named Hjalmar, who would have attacked Bond riding on an elephant.

Later in the story, after being double-crossed by Blofeld with synthetic diamonds, Sten offers to help Bond take down Blofeld as they have a common goal. This sees Bond teaming with Hjalmar, who earlier tried to eliminate him. Bond and Hjalmar follow Blofeld's trail to a floating palace à la *Octopussy* where they meet Blofeld's mistress, named Jadaputta. Bond finds Blofeld there, too, and shoots him. But, in what turns out to be a precursor to the finished film's pre-credit sequence, it was just a hyper-realistic effigy of Blofeld. Afterwards, Hjalmar double-crosses 007—never a good idea—and Bond kills him.

Bond then stows away on one of Sten's planes, which lands on a supertanker called the *SS Cassiopia*.[162] The rather messy treatment, overcrowded with two main villains, gets messier from there. Basically, Sten has been using the diamonds to create a super satellite, complete with a laser.[163] Said laser is not for simple destructive purposes, but espionage as the laser allows for a type of

---

[161] As an alternative, Maibaum considered Adamas Oganston which would roughly translate to "Diamondfinger" which may have been too on the nose.

[162] It's likely that Goldfinger's supertanker was lifted from Gerry Anderson's *Moonraker* script, which was one of the projects considered to follow *OHMSS*.

[163] Don't forget, Auric Goldfinger did have an affinity for lasers as evidenced by the one he almost cut Bond in half with.

1970s-era computer hacking...somehow. Blofeld has been supplying Sten with the diamonds, knowing full well of Sten's goal. As such, Blofeld wants to let Sten build the satellite so he can steal it and then use it himself. Bond informs Sten of this, then escapes the supertanker by hijacking a plane and flying off to M. In doing so, he leaves Tiffany Case behind so she can play damsel in distress for the climax.

Actually, said climax is very much like1977's *The Spy Who Loved Me*, with Bond boarding a submarine that torpedoes the supertanker. Bond would then enter the sinking ship to save Tiffany, while the Russians take down Sten's satellite in space. Sten simply goes down with his ship, and Bond and Tiffany swim to a floating escape pod only to find it's already occupied by Wint, Kidd and Blofeld. Overcrowded literally and figuratively, the story would end with a fight in the cramped quarters of the pod. Bond kills Wint and Kidd, while Blofeld gets fed to the sharks.

A revised treatment utilized many of the same story beats, though this one had Bond meeting Sten's two mistresses who he may or may not have had an offscreen threesome with. (One could argue the same was implied with the two gypsy women in *From Russia with Love*.) The next day, Bond meets Sten, who is the spitting image of Goldfinger, only his hair is pure white, probably to tie in with the diamond theme. Hjalmar returns as Sten's henchman, but is envisioned by Maibaum as a female-to-male transgender character.

This treatment better addresses the relationship between Sten and Bond regarding Goldfinger. Sten takes note of Bond's recognizing him, and simply deducts that Bond must have met his brother. Bond's simple response is that the two played golf together once. Sten has no love for his brother, and remarks to Bond that "Mother always said [Auric] was a bit retarded." Furthermore, Sten claims he wants to rehabilitate the family image after Auric's stupid plot to blow up Fort Knox. In the classic Bond tradition, 007 engages in a game with Sten: that of a backgammon game made of diamonds. In a precursor to a similar outcome in *Octopussy*, Bond uses Sten's own loaded dice against him to win the game. The treatment ends the same way as the previous one on a sinking tanker. Blofeld gets thrown to the sharks again, only with a caveat to not see Blofeld getting eaten just in case the producers ever wanted to bring him back again.

Gert Fröbe, who portrayed Goldfinger in the 1964 film, was still friendly with Saltzman and Broccoli in 1971, and some have said that he wasn't opposed to the idea of returning. The same source implied that Fröbe's schedule simply didn't permit his return, and so it was axed. It's just as likely, though, that the idea was discarded before Fröbe could even be asked.

BIBLIOGRAPHY

Books

Archer, Simon and Stan Nicholls. *Gerry Anderson: The Authorized Biography*. LEGEND, 1996.

Chancellor, Henry. *James Bond: The Man and His World*. John Murray Publishers, 2005.

Duncan, Paul. *The James Bond Archives*. Taschen America LLC., 2023.

Edlitz, Mark. *The Lost Adventures of James Bond: Timothy Dalton's Third and Fourth Bond Films, James Bond Jr., and Other Unmade or Forgotten 007 Projects*. By the author, 2020.

Feutry, Clément. *Scripting 007: Behind the Writing of the James Bond Movies*. By the author, 2024.

Fleming, Fergus. *The Man with the Golden Typewriter: Ian Fleming's James Bond Letters*. Bloomsbury, 2016.

Lycett, Andrew. *Ian Fleming*. St. Martin's Press, 2013.

Macintyre, Ben. *For Your Eyes Only: Ian Fleming and James Bond.* Bloomsbury Publishing PLC, 2009.

Mankiewicz, Tom and Robert Crane. *My Life as a Mankiewicz: An Insider's Journey through Hollywood*. University Press of Kentucky, 2012.

Parker, Matthew. *Goldeneye: Where James Bond Was Born: Ian Fleming's Jamaica*. Pegasus Books, 2016.

Pearson, John. *The Life of Ian Fleming*. Bloomsbury Reader, 2013.

Pfeifer, Lee and Philip Lisa. *The Incredible World of 007: An Authorized Celebration of James Bond*. Citadel Press, 1995.

Articles

Duns, Jeremy. "*Casino Royale*: discovering the lost script." *Telegraph* (March 2, 2011).

Hellman, Geoffrey T. "Bond's Creator." *The New Yorker* (April 21, 1962).

Nudd, John. "Ian Fleming & James Bond." *The Book and Magazine Collector* (October 1989).

O'Brien, Steve. "James Bond: Details of Gerry Anderson's unmade *Moonraker* movie revealed." Yahoo!movies (April 2023).

Videos

Cork, John (writer/director). *Inside Live and Let Die*. MGM Home Entertainment, 1999.

INDEX

ABOUT THE AUTHOR

John LeMay is a lifelong James Bond fan and the author of over fifty published books, many of them film histories. Among his better-known works are *Jaws Unmade: The Lost Sequels, Prequels, Remakes, and Rip-Offs*; *Kong Unmade: The Lost Films of Skull Island*; and *Trailing the Pink Panther Films: An Unauthorized Guide to the Pink Panther Series.* For several years, LeMay was the editor and publisher of *The Lost Films Fanzine*, and has written for publications like *Cinema Retro*, *Xenorama*, *Castle of Frankenstein*, and other film-centric publications. LeMay is also the author of the adventure novels *The Noted Desperado Pancho Dumez*; *Once Upon a Time in Fort Sumner*; and *Billy the Kid & the Ballad of the Boy Bandit King.*

THE BICEP BOOKS CATALOGUE

The following titles are available for purchase on Amazon.com, and are available to bookstores at a wholesale discount via Ingram Content Group (ISBNs of available editions listed for this purpose)

THE BIG BOOK OF JAPANESE GIANT MONSTER MOVIES SERIES

The third edition of the book that started it all! Reviews over 100 tokusatsu films between 1954 and 1988. All the Godzilla, Gamera, and Daimajin movies made during the Showa era are covered plus lesser known fare like *Invisible Man vs. The Human Fly* (1957) and *Conflagration* (1975). Softcover (380 pp/5.83" X 8.27") Suggested Retail: $19.99 SBN:978-1-7341546 -4-1

This third edition reviews over 75 tokusatsu films between 1989 and 2019. All the Godzilla, Gamera, and Ultraman movies made during the Heisei era are covered plus independent films like *Reigo, King of the Sea Monsters* (2005), *Demeking, the Sea Monster* (2009) and *Attack of the Giant Teacher* (2019)! Softcover (260 pp/5.83" X 8.27") Suggested Retail: $19.99 ISBN: 978-1- 7347816-4-9

This second edition of the Rondo Award nominated book covers un-produced scripts like *Bride of Godzilla* (1955), partially shot movies like *Giant Horde Beast Nezura* (1963), and banned films like *Prophecies of Nostradamus* (1974), plus hundreds of other lost productions. Soft-cover/Hard-cover (470pp. /7" X 10") Suggested Retail: $24.99 (sc)/$39.95(hc)ISBN: 978-1-73 41546-0-3 (hc)

This sequel to *The Lost Films* covers the non-giant monster unmade movie scripts from Japan such as *Frankenstein vs. the Human Vapor* (1963), *After Japan Sinks* (1974-76), plus lost movies like *Fearful Attack of the Flying Saucers* (1956) and *Venus Flytrap* (1968). Hardcover (200 pp/5.83" X 8.27")/Softcover (216 pp/ 5.5" X 8.5") Suggested Retail: $9.99 (sc)/$24.99(hc) ISBN:978-1-7341546 -3-4 (hc)

This companion book to *The Lost Films* charts the development of all the prominent Japanese monster movies including discarded screenplays, story ideas, and deleted scenes. Also includes bios for writers like Shinichi Sekizawa, Niisan Takahashi and many others. Comprehensive script listing and appendices as well. Hardcover/Softcover (370 pp./ 6"X9") Suggested Retail: $16.95(sc)/$34.99(hc)ISBN: 978-1-7341546-5-8 (hc)

Examines the differences between the U.S. and Japanese versions of over 50 different tokusatsu films like *Gojira* (1954)/*Godzilla, King of the Monsters!* (1956), *Gamera* (1965)/ *Gammera, the Invincible* (1966), *Submersion of Japan* (1973)/*Tidal Wave* (1975), and many, many more! Softcover (540 pp./ 6"X9") Suggested Retail: $22.99 ISBN: 978-1-953221-77 -3

Examines the differences between the European and Japanese versions of tokusatsu films including the infamous "Cozzilla" colorized version of *Godzilla*, from 1977, plus rarities like *Terremoto 10 Grado*, the Italian cut of *Legend of Dinosaurs*. The book also examines the condensed Champion Matsuri edits of Toho's effects films. Softcover (372 pp./ 6"X9") Suggested Retail: $19.99 ISBN: 978-1- 953221-77-3

HUMOR

Throughout the 1960s and 1970s the Italian film industry cranked out over 600 "Spaghetti Westerns" and for every *Fistful of Dollars* were a dozen pale imitations, some of them hilarious. Many of these lesser known Spaghettis are available in bargain bin DVD packs and stream for free online. If ever you've wondered which are worth your time and which aren't, this is the book for you. Softcover (160pp./5.06" X 7.8") Suggested Retail: $9.99

THE BICEP BOOKS CATALOGUE

CLASSIC MONSTERS SERIES

Kong Unmade explores unproduced scripts like *King Kong vs. Frankenstein* (1958), unfinished films like *The Lost Island* (1934), and lost movies like *King Kong Appears in Edo* (1938). As a bonus, all the Kong rip-offs like *Konga* (1961) and *Queen Kong* (1976) are reviewed. Hardcover (350 pp/5.83" X 8.27")/Softcover (376 pp/ 5.5" X 8.5") Suggested Retail: $24.99 (hc)/$19.99(sc) ISBN: 978-1-7341546-2-7(hc)

Jaws Unmade explores unproduced scripts like *Jaws 3, People 0* (1979), abandoned ideas like a Quint prequel, and even aborted sequels to Jaws inspired movies like *Orca Part II*. As a bonus, all the Jaws rip-offs like *Grizzly* (1976) and *Tentacles* (1977) are reviewed. Hardcover (316 pp/5.83" X 8.27")/Softcover (340 pp/5.5" X 8.5") Suggested Retail: $29.99 (hc)/$17.95(sc) ISBN: 978-1-7344730-1-8

Classic Monsters Unmade covers lost and unmade films starring Dracula, Frankenstein, the Mummy and more monsters. Reviews unmade scripts like *The Return of Frankenstein* (1934) and *Wolf Man vs. Dracula* (1944). It also examines lost films of the silent era such as *The Werewolf* (1913) and *Drakula's Death* (1923). Softcover/ Hardcover(428pp/5.83"X8.27") Suggested Retail: $22.99(sc)/ $27.99(hc)ISBN:978-1- 953221-85-8(hc)

Volume 2 explores the Hammer era and beyond, from unmade versions of *Brides of Dracula* (called *Disciple of Dracula*) to remakes of *Creature from the Black Lagoon*. Completely unmade films like *Kali: Devil Bride of Dracula* (1975) and *Godzilla vs. Frankenstein* (1964) are covered along with lost completed films like *Batman Fights Dracula* (1967) and *Black the Ripper* (1974). Coming Fall 2021.

NOSTALGIA

Written in the same spirit as *The Big Book of Japanese Giant Monster Movies*, this tome reviews all the classic Universal and Hammer horrors to star Dracula, Frankenstein, the Gillman and the rest along with obscure flicks like *The New Invisible Man* (1958), *Billy the Kid versus Dracula* (1966), *Blackenstein* (1973) and *Legend of the Werewolf* (1974). Softcover (394 pp/5.5" X 8.5") Suggested Retail: $17.95

Written at an intermediate reading level for the kid in all of us, these picture books will take you back to your youth. In the spirit of the old Ian Thorne books are covered *Nabonga* (1944), *White Pongo* (1945) and more! Hardcover/Softcover (44 pp/7.5" X 9.25") Suggested Retail: $17.95(hc)/$9.99(sc) ISBN: 978- 1-7341546-9-6 (hc) 978- 1-7344730-5-6 (sc)

Written at an intermediate reading level for the kid in all of us, these picture books will take you back to your youth. In the spirit of the old Ian Thorne books are covered *The Lost World* (1925), *The Land That Time Forgot* (1975) and more! Hardcover/Softcover (44 pp/7.5" X 9.25") Suggested Retail: $17.95 (hc)/$9.99(sc) ISBN: 978-1-7344730 -6-3 (hc) 978- 1-7344730-7-0 (sc)

Written at an intermediate reading level for the kid in all of us, these picture books will take you back to your youth. In the spirit of the old Ian Thorne books are covered *Them!* (1954), *Empire of the Ants* (1977) and more! Hardcover/ Softcover (44 pp/7.5" X 9.25") Suggested Retail: $17.95(hc)/ $9.99(sc) ISBN: 978-1-7347816 -3-2 (hc) 978 -1-7347816-2-5 (sc)

THE BICEP BOOKS CATALOGUE

The following titles are available for purchase on Amazon.com, and are available to bookstores at a wholesale discount via Ingram Content Group (ISBNs of available editions listed for this purpose)

CRYPTOZOOLOGY/COWBOYS & SAURIANS

Cowboys & Saurians: Prehistoric Beasts as Seen by the Pioneers explores dinosaur sightings from the pioneer period via real newspaper reports from the time. Well-known cases like the Tombstone Thunderbird are covered along with more obscure cases like the Crosswicks Monster and more. Softcover (357 pp/5.06" X 7.8") Suggested Retail: $19.95 ISBN: 978-1-7341546-1-0

Cowboys & Saurians: Ice Age zeroes in on snowbound saurians like the Ceratosaurus of the Arctic Circle and a Tyrannosaurus of the Tundra, as well as sightings of Ice Age megafauna like mammoths, glyptodonts, Sarkastodons and Saber-toothed tigers. Tales of a land that time forgot in the Arctic are also covered. Softcover (264 pp/5.06" X 7.8") Suggested Retail: $14.99 ISBN: 978-1-7341546-7-2

Southerners & Saurians takes the series formula of exploring newspaper accounts of monsters in the pioneer period with an eye to the Old South. In addition to dinosaurs are covered Lizardmen, Frogmen, giant leeches and mosquitoes, and the Dingocroc, which might be an alien rather than a prehistoric survivor. Softcover (202 pp/5.06" X 7.8") Suggested Retail: $13.99 ISBN: 978-1-7344730-4-9

Cowboys & Saurians South of the Border explores the saurians of Central and South America, like the Patagonian Plesiosaurus that was really an Iemisch, plus tales of the Neo-Mylodon, a menacing monster from underground called the Minhocao, Glyptodonts, and even Bolivia's three-headed dinosaur! Softcover (412 pp/ 5.06"X7.8") Suggested Retail: $17.95 ISBN: 978-1-953221-73-5

UFOLOGY/THE REAL COWBOYS & ALIENS IN CONJUNCTION WITH ROSWELL BOOKS

The Real Cowboys and Aliens: Early American UFOs explores UFO sightings in the USA between the years 1800-1864. Stories of encounters sometimes involved famous figures in U.S. history such as Lewis and Clark, and Thomas Jefferson.Hardcover (242pp/6" X 9") Softcover (262 pp/5.06" X 7.8") Suggested Retail: $24.99 (hc)/$15.95(sc) ISBN: 978-1-7341546-8-9\(hc)/978-1-7344730-8-7(sc)

The second entry in the series, *Old West UFOs*, covers reports spanning the years 1865-1895. Includes tales of Men in Black, Reptilians, Spring-Heeled Jack, Sasquatch from space, and other alien beings, in addition to the UFOs and airships. Hardcover (276 pp/6" X 9") Softcover (308 pp/5.06" X 7.8") Suggested Retail: $29.95 (hc)/$17.95(sc) ISBN: 978-1-7344730-0-1 (hc)/ 978-1-7344730-2-5 (sc)

The third entry in the series, *The Coming of the Airships*, encompasses a short time frame with an incredibly high concentration of airship sightings between 1896-1899. The famous Aurora, Texas, UFO crash of 1897 is covered in depth along with many others. Hardcover (196 pp/6" X 9") Softcover (222 pp/5.06" X 7.8") Suggested Retail: $24.99 (hc)/$15.95(sc) ISBN: 978-1-7347816-1-8 (hc)/978-1-7347816-0-1(sc)

Featuring cases the authors missed, *The Lost Cases* covers things such as the skyquakes recorded by Lewis and Clark, airships and the Spanish American War, Pancho Villa and crystal skulls, lost alien tribe of the Tundra, invisible alien monsters, the Great Moon Hoax of 1835, hellhounds and airships, the Sonora Airship Club and more. Softcover (252 pp/5.06" X 7.8") Suggested Retail: $18.99 ISBN: 978-1-953221-55-1

BICEP BOOKS HISTORY

COWBOYS & SAURIANS CONT'D

Cowboys & Saurians: Dinosaurs Down Under takes the series to Australia to explore tales of the cattle devouring Burrunjor, the dreaded Diprotodon, the terrible Tantanoola Tiger, the marsupial Sasquatch known as the Yowie, plus Thylacines, Bunyips, giant rabbits, Megalodons and dinosaurs in nearby New Zealand. Softcover (240 pp/ 5.06" X 7.8") Suggested Retail: $14.95 ISBN: 978-1-953221-34-6

As the title suggest, *Cowboys & Saurians in the Modern Era* takes the series into the 20th Century with tales of the Texas Pterosaur flap of 1976, the Bladenboro Beast of the 1950s, the Busco Turtle Beast of the 1940s, dinosaur sightings in the Great Depression and far out tales of mini-mastodons, dinosaur men, and Snallygasters. Softcover (320 pp/ 5.06" X 7.8") Suggested Retail: $19.95 ISBN: 978-1-953221-22-3

Settlers & Serpents wrangles the best "Snaik Stories" of the Southwest and beyond in a single volume. Whether it's simple giant snakes or lake serpents, they're corralled in the pages within. Also included are entries on the Leviathan in Mesoamerica and the Southwest plus a detailed look at the giant rattlesnake of Pecos Pueblo. Softcover (180 pp/ 5.06" X 7.8") Suggested Retail: $14.99 ISBN: 978-1-953221-21-6

Written for young readers ages 9-12, *Monsters of the Old South* collects the best creature stories of the swamplands including the White River Monster, Green Eyes, the Crocodingo, the Averasboro Gallinipper, the Tennessee Snake Woman, the Arkansas Gowrow, Bigfoot in the Mississippi River and more. Softcover (122 pp/4.25" X 7") Suggested Retail: $12.99 ISBN: 978-17347816-9-4

THE REAL COWBOYS & ALIENS CONT'D

Early 20th Century UFOs kicks off a new series that investigates UFO sightings of the early 1900s. Includes tales of UFOs sighted over the *Titanic* as it sunk, Nikola Tesla receiving messages from the stars, an alien being found encased in ice, and a possible virus from outer space!Hardcover (196 pp/6" X 9") Softcover (222 pp/5.06" X 7.8") Suggested Retail: $27.99 (hc)/$16.95(sc) ISBN: 978-1-7347816-1-8 (hc)/978-1-7347816-0-1(sc)

UFOs in the Roaring Twenties takes a look at UFO sightings in the 1920s just as the title suggests, along with accounts of Mothman in Nebraska, Lincoln LaPaz's first UFO case, Men in Black investigating an airship crash in Braxton County, West Virginia, Camden's Cosmic Sniper, and much more! Softcover (248 pp/5.06" X 7.8") Suggested Retail: $19.99 ISBN: 978-1-953221-51-3

UFOs of the Turbulent Thirties concludes the authors' investigation of the last unexplored decade of Ufology in the Great Depression with accounts of Mothman, Ghost Fliers, Nazi Bells, the Underground City of the Lizard People, a vanished village on the tundra, and even gangsters and aliens. Softcover (212 pp/5.06" X 7.8") Suggested Retail: $17.95 ISBN: 978-1-953221-35-3

Written for young readers ages 9-12, *Space Monsters of the Old West* collects the best alien sightings of the Wild West including Mummies from Mars, Bigfoot from the Moon, Pascagoula's space ghouls, the Crawfordsville Monster, Spring-Heeled Jack, Blobs from space, and even the dinosaurian alien creatures that invaded Van Meter, Iowa. Softcover (120 pp/4.25" X 7") Suggested Retail: $12.99 ISBN: 978-1-953221-87-2

BICEP BOOKS HISTORY

COWBOYS & MONSTERS

Cowboys & Monsters features potentially true stories of real vampires, werewolves, and even mummies unique to America's Wild West period. Examples include the cursed mummy of John Wilkes Booth, New Orleans immortal vampire Jacques St. Germain, precursors to the Beast of Bray Road, and the origins of Skinwalker Ranch. Softcover (316 pp/5.06" X 7.8") Suggested Retail: $19.99 ISBN: 978-1-953221-46-9

The first entry in this trilogy of non-fiction terror sinks its teeth into the lore of the vampire in North America and Mexico, with detailed rundowns on the vampire hunters of Exeter, Rhode Island, a tribe of Bat People, the nocturnal shape-shifting vampire witches of Tlaxcala, the immortal ways of Comte St. Germain in New Orleans and more. Softcover (200 pp/ 5.06" X 7.8") Suggested Retail: $12.99 ISBN: 978-1-953221-38-4

Mummies of the Americas explores Death Valley's city of the Dead, King Tut's Tomb along the Arkansas, the Egyptian City of the Grand Canyon plus the famous mummies of John Wilkes Boothe, Elmer McCurdy, the Cardiff Giant, the Mummy of Helldorado, and even Billy the Kid's pickled trigger finger! Softcover (200 pp/5.06" X 7.8") Suggested Retail: $12.99 ISBN: 978-1-953221-37-7

Cowboys & Dogmen is devoted to tales of werewolves of the Wild West including the dreaded Navajo skinwalker, the Watrous Werewolf, the Beast of the Land Between Lakes, the Hellhounds of El Dorado Canyon, the dreaded Dog Eater, the Wahhoo, the Wolf Man of Versailles, the Michigan Dog-Man and more! Softcover (212 pp/5.06" X 7.8") Suggested Retail: $12.99 ISBN: 978-1-953221-36-0

FICTION/ MISC. HISTORY

The first novel from historian John LeMay weaves a fantastic web of fiction via real life mysteries and legends of New Mexico, namely the puzzling theft and return of Billy the Kid's tombstone in 1976, the legend of the Lost Adams Diggings, the villainous Santa Fe Ring, and the enigmatic Acoma Mesa. Softcover (250 pp/5.5" X 7.5") Suggested Retail: $14.95 ISBN: 978-1-953221-42-1

The year is 1950, and old timers connected to the long-dead outlaw Billy the Kid are turning up murdered in New Mexico. Some blame the killings on the avenging witch of the Navajo nation, the skinwalker, while others think it's no coincidence that a man claiming to be a surviving Billy the Kid is set to meet with the governor soon... Softcover (260 pp/5.5" X 7.5") Suggested Retail: $16.95 ISBN: 978-1-953221-32-2

Roswell, USA, the long-forgotten debut work of John LeMay, is available again and covers the minutia of the infamous Roswell UFO Crash of 1947. Notable chapters include tales of an alien ghost haunting the old airbase, monsters in the nearby Bottomless Lakes, and even a dinosaur sighting outside of town. Softcover (248 pp/6" X 9") Suggested Retail: $14.95 ISBN: 978-0-9817597-5-3

This biography, for the first time ever, tells the history of western journalist Ash Upson, who ghostwrote Pat Garrett's *The Authentic Life of Billy the Kid* in 1882 and also reproduces many of Upson's letters that detailed the harsh realities of frontier life in New Mexico during the turbulent Lincoln County War. Softcover (318 pp/5.5" X 8.5") Suggested Retail: $16.99 ISBN: 978-1953221919